WHISPERS AT THE PAGODA

ASIAN
PORTRAITS

VISAGES
D'ASIE

WHISPERS AT THE PAGODA

PORTRAITS OF MODERN BURMA

Julie Sell

Orchid Press
Bangkok 1999

Julie Sell:

WHISPERS AT THE PAGODA
PORTRAITS OF MODERN BURMA

Orchid Press
98/13 Soi Apha Phirom, Ratchada Road,
Chatuchak, Bangkok 10900, Thailand

ISBN 974-8304-36-1

*T*he preamble of the Universal Declaration proclaims the "advent of a world in which human beings shall enjoy freedom of speech and belief and freedom from fear and want" to be the "highest aspiration of the common people". It is also the most basic need for all, regardless of race, religion or nationality. Our struggle for human rights has brought us very close to all members of the human family who are striving for the recognition of their inherent dignity and their inalienable right to life, liberty and security of person.

It is my hope that our common aims and sufferings will create a strong sense of solidarity that surpasses national frontiers and cultural differences. We struggle with a sense of purpose and an unshakable faith in the power of compassion and endeavor and universal brotherhood. As our gratitude goes out to those who have supported us so generously in our times of adversity, we would like to express the hope that one day, soon, our country too may be a source of strength and support for those in need of peace, justice and freedom.

— Aung San Suu Kyi, Nobel Peace Laureate and General Secretary of Burma's National League for Democracy, on December 10, 1998, the 50th Anniversary of the Universal Declaration of Human Rights.

Contents

Preface

This book is about people in a little-known Asian country that has been overlooked by much of the world. They are warm and welcoming people with ancient traditions and a pride in their culture, but everyday life is a struggle for them in this land of harsh realities. Worrying that the world has forgotten them, they long to speak out freely, yet fear the consequences of doing so. This book aims to make their voices heard.

Relatively little has been written about Burma[1] in recent years, due to the country's self-imposed isolation for more than three decades. It has not always been that way. As a steamy outpost of the British Empire in the early twentieth century, Burma was a source of inspiration for numerous writers, including Rudyard Kipling and George Orwell. Ever since a military coup in 1962, however, much of what happens inside Burma has been a mystery to the outside world. For those that have had a peek inside, it has been tempting to focus on one dramatic extreme or another in this land of paradoxes, which is wedged between the great land masses of China and India.

On one hand there is the delightful and alluring Burma, a lush tropical country of saffron-robed monks, sparkling pagodas, and the crumbling charm of old Asia. The images are a photographer's dream: centuries-old temples, colorful Buddhist festivals, working elephants, and shy tribespeople in traditional costumes at the upcountry markets. I have heard more than one foreign tourist exclaim that Burma is the most charming place they have ever visited. This 'public' face of the country is being promoted by a government that has cautiously cracked the doors open to tourism in recent years, under the conditions that visitors bring plenty of foreign currency, never stray from 'unrestricted' zones, and avoid too much interaction with the local people.

Well-hidden from the view of tourists is the other, darker side of Burma. The military junta has changed its name several times since 1962 – most recently, the much-maligned State Law and Order Restoration Council (SLORC) was rechristened the State Peace and Development Council

---

[1] The use of 'Burma', rather than 'Myanmar', in reference to the country reflects not only the long use and broader name recognition of Burma around the world (it was officially changed to Myanmar in 1989), but also the fact that the extremely unpopular military government is the chief proponent of the use of the name Myanmar. In addition, the name Myanmar is rejected by many ethnic minority groups since it was the name given historically to the country by the Burman ethnic majority. The opposition National League for Democracy still refers to the country as Burma.

(SPDC) in 1997 – but essentially the same policies have prevailed. International human rights groups and political activists frequently cite the
Burmese government for its abysmal human rights record, putting the
junta in the same category as the regimes in Iraq, Afghanistan, and
North Korea. An uphill struggle for democracy has been underway in
the country for years, led since 1988 by the Nobel Peace Prize winner
Aung San Suu Kyi, who served six years under house arrest and is still
severely restricted by the authorities. Hundreds of her supporters have
been jailed and harassed.

In the mountainous regions that ring Burma like a horseshoe, an
assortment of minority ethnic groups, many of which have sought autonomy or at least equal rights from the central government, are subject
to the forced relocation of their villages, forced labor, extortion, and
often killings and rape at the hands of the army. In addition, massive
military spending and mismanagement have put the country in dire economic straits (quite a feat, since Burma has been blessed by nature with
abundant resources including teak, jade, rubies, oil, gas, and fertile soil
for growing). Finally, the government has a stranglehold on the flow of
people and information in the country. In short, Burma has such a startling array of problems that it would be easy to dismiss as just another
Third World basket case.

But the people of Burma deserve to have their stories told. This book
aims to look beneath the shiny surface of spruced up pagodas and the
grim catalog of human rights abuses, in order to put a human face on
Burma. As you come to know the people of Burma through these stories, I hope that you will be simultaneously captivated, intrigued, and
saddened, as I was.

I did not intend to write a book when I first went to Burma several
years ago. I was a former journalist who had worked and traveled widely
in Asia, and was eager to discover a little-known country with a controversial reputation. I made that first trip with a French journalist friend,
who, like me, had spent a lot of time in the hot and dusty corners of the
world. We both knew that Burma's military government was not keen
on journalists or writers, even those on holiday, so we kept low profiles
and stuck to the handful of cities that are officially open to foreigners.
We could not escape our innate curiosity, however, and over the course
of a few weeks in the country, we found ourselves seeking out conversations with the locals whenever possible. The fact that I was American
was particularly fascinating to the Burmese[2], and they seemed awed by

---

[2] The adjective 'Burmese' is used in reference to things in the country of Burma, including
the people. 'Burman' refers to a specific ethnic group, which makes up the majority of the
Burmese population.

my blond curls and blue eyes. Their innocent curiosity won us over immediately.

Despite our hopes to understand more about how individual lives were affected by the government, however, most of the conversations we had with local people on that first trip never went beyond polite exchanges, even in the few instances when we were invited into people's homes. When individuals hesitantly offered a few words about the country's political situation on occasion, the other family members or friends present usually looked down or started shifting about uncomfortably until the subject was changed.

The Burmese government has made a concerted effort to keep meaningful contact between the local people and foreigners to a minimum, apparently out of concern that the population will be exposed to dangerous ideas and be stirred to action. The secret police seem to have a nearly airtight web of informants in place that heightens the sense of fear, and few local residents will venture into more than polite, brief conversation with visitors. So widespread is their caution that the name of opposition leader Aung San Suu Kyi, if mentioned at all, is only whispered in public. On a number of occasions, when speaking with local people about nothing more than sites of cultural interest, I saw them glance over their shoulders for fear of attracting attention.

It was the official desire to keep me at a distance from the Burmese people that made me all the more determined to get to know them. As this book took shape, my primary goal was to capture the stories of a diverse group of individuals throughout Burma that would personalize broader issues in the country, and to present them in a form that would be accessible to general readers.

The encounters and stories in this book did not occur in any particular sequence. They were gathered over the course of several trips to the country in the mid- to late-1990s. In many instances, I went back to see people more than once. Some of the encounters happened by chance, others were arranged by friends when I expressed interest in a particular aspect of Burmese life or in a person who seemed particularly worth meeting.

Because these experiences came to me in fairly random sequence, I debated how to present them in a book. A chronology did not seem to make sense. Ultimately, I decided to group together experiences by general theme, and to present them in sections that have common threads running throughout them.

There are four parts to this book. Part I, called 'Echoes of 1988', is the most political section of the book. It tells the stories of people whose lives were permanently altered by the democracy movement of 1988 that was violently crushed by the military. A number of the people whose stories I tell are still intimately involved in the struggle. They include the opposition leader Aung San Suu Kyi (one of only two people whose real names are used in this book), as well as former student leaders of the democracy movement. The stories of writers and other intellectuals who have been targeted by the regime are also told here.

Part II, called 'Tradition', focuses on the rich cultural aspects of life in Burma. The voices in this section talk about the pervasive influence of Buddhism on daily life, attempts to revive traditional performing arts, and remnants of the British colonial era. Many of the most alluring aspects of Burma today stem from its colorful past.

Part III, 'Today's Struggles', contains stories about issues that tear at people's lives today. These include a view of the military from a long-time soldier's perspective, the tale of a rural headman whose village had to perform forced labor, stories from some of the ethnic minorities who have fled repression and attacks by the military in remote border states, and the struggles of doctors seeking to provide health care in a country that has one of the world's fastest-growing rates of AIDS.

Part IV is entitled 'Voices of Tomorrow'. This section of the book focuses on stories of the younger generation that is changing the face of the country. It includes discussions of the growing Chinese influence in Burma, illustrated through a young woman's tale, and with students of all ages who aspire to better lives.

A number of the people who shared their stories with me are quite famous in Burma, but most are common people. Out of concern for their safety, none of our extended conversations were held in public. Amazingly, only one person who was due to meet me failed to arrive for our appointment, for fear of being seen with a foreigner. But on a number of occasions, individuals who had been imprisoned or harassed by the government in the past made exceptional efforts to cooperate with me, at potentially significant risk to themselves. Many spoke very carefully – literally in whispers – about the current situation in their country.

I was constantly aware of the need to avoid attracting attention that might bring harm to the people I met with. My caution was heightened by Western diplomats I spoke with in Rangoon, who warned that I should not mention local people's names on the telephone, since the calls from my hotel room were likely being recorded. They also encouraged me to send my research notes and film out of the country with other foreigners, in case I was stopped and searched by the authorities as a result of interviews with opposition political figures. I heeded the warnings, and made every effort to appear as just another tourist. I frequently wondered if I was being overly paranoid, but my friends and diplomatic contacts in Burma assured me the caution was warranted.

Often when I thanked the local people for their willingness to share stories with me, they shook their heads. 'Thank you for your interest,' more than one person said to me. 'We want the world to know about Burma.' It was a sentiment that kept me pressing forward with this project.

Several people particularly inspired me as I researched this book. One of them was an elderly woman with fire in her eyes and a will of iron. I made several trips to see Daw Khin Mu (the honorific Daw means 'aunt' and is widely used to address adult women) during my time in Burma. We sat in rattan chairs by a window in her high-ceilinged living room, facing each other and fanning ourselves in the heat. Like any grandmother, she would always ply me with food and drink, usually short, plump bananas and a cup of hot tea. Unlike most grandmothers I know, however, she also took care to close the shutters each time we sat down, lest any eavesdroppers be lingering outside her window.

During several afternoons together, Daw Khin Mu told me stories from her long, full life. They were heart-wrenching tales of war, repression, imprisonment, death, and suffering for members of her family. She, her husband, and children have endured decades of physical and emotional hardship. After hearing the stories, I was in awe that Daw Khin Mu retained such a kind face and a generous heart. With her children and grandchildren living around her, she appeared to have found a measure of peace and contentment.

One day when I went to visit her, she had just returned from the Buddhist monastery where her grandson was initiated as a novice monk, and she glowed as any proud grandmother would. Yet once we sat down to talk, her fire quickly returned.

'After all our country and our people have been through over the years, this time is the worst,' she told me. 'The economic situation is taking a toll. People are working harder and harder for less and less. In many families, both the husband and wife work two jobs each to make ends meet. It is putting a strain on families. Some people are going hungry. But the worst pressure we face is political.' As did so many whose voices are heard in this book, Daw Khin Mu urged me to share the stories of people who have been silenced by fear.

'We Burmese are always like this,' she said, pointing a finger at her temple, as if a gun were pressed to her head. 'We cannot say anything. We cannot write anything freely. The government holds everything in its hand, and it will give nothing up. Only those on the outside can say something about this situation.'

It is a situation worth understanding. As you will see in the following pages, Burma is a country rich in humanity that survives under the harshest of government systems. I hope the individual stories contained in this book will provide a deeper understanding of a country that is at once alluring, tragic and complex.

With the exceptions of Aung San Suu Kyi and Dr Cynthia Maung, all names in this book have been changed to protect the people who assisted me. Similarly, none of the people whose individual stories I relate, with the exception of Aung San Suu Kyi and Dr Cynthia Maung, appear in the photographs in this book.

Acknowledgements

This book was inspired and made possible by the people of Burma. Their generosity and courage has touched me and regularly reminded me of the strength of the human spirit. Unfortunately they must go unnamed here, for their own safety and welfare. I would also like to thank my overseas Burmese friends and the Burma scholars who supported this project by helping me make contact with individuals inside Burma, as well as providing guidance and feedback on the manuscript. Thanks to Hal Kuløy for his encouragement and good humor throughout the entire development and production process, and to Tom Riddle and David Murray for their careful work on the final text and book design in Bangkok. Dominic Faulder and another photographer who chooses to remain unidentified gave added dimension to the book through their images. Friends and colleagues throughout the U.S., Europe, and Asia showed an interest in the subject that encouraged me to push forward at times when I began to doubt the viability of the project. Finally, I would like to thank my family for their love, support and acceptance of my sometimes prolonged "disappearances" inside Burma while researching this book.

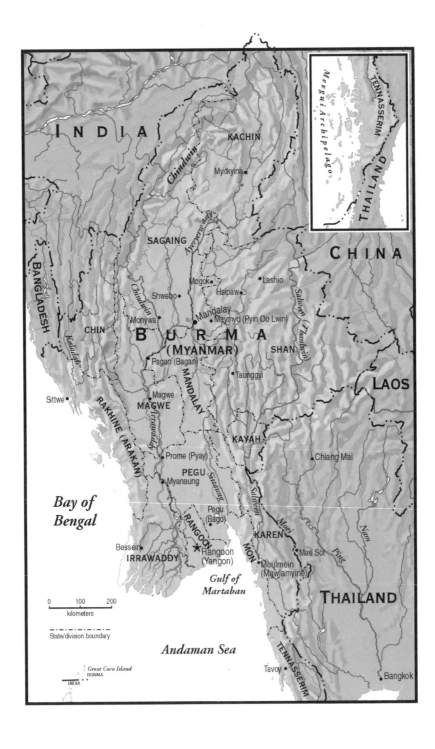

INDIA

KACHIN

Chindwin

Myitkyina •

Ayeyarwaddy

SAGAING

CHINA

Mogok • • Lashio

Chindwin

Shwebo • Hsipaw •

Salween (Thanlwin)

Monywa • Mandalay
• Maymyo (Pyin Oo Lwin)

BURMA
(MYANMAR)

SHAN

Pagan (Bagan) •

Kaladan

CHIN

• Taunggyi

LAOS

Sittwe •

MANDALAY

Magwe •
MAGWE

Irrawaddy

KAYAH

Prome (Pyay) •

• Chiang Mai

RAKHINE (ARAKAN)

PEGU
• Myanaung

Sittaung

**Bay of
Bengal**

Pegu
(Bago) •

Salween

KAREN

RANGOON

Bessein •
IRRAWADDY

★ Rangoon
(Yangon)

MON

Moulmein
(Mawlamyine) •

Moei

• Mae Sot

Ping

Nam

THAILAND

**Gulf of
Martaban**

0   100   200
└──┴──┴──┘
kilometers

State/division boundary

Andaman Sea

⌀ *Great Coco Island*
BURMA
─────────
INDIA ⚬ ⚬

TENNASSERIM

Tavoy •

• Bangkok

Mergui Archipelago

TENNASSERIM

THAILAND

Part I
Echoes of 1988

Chapter 1

A View From The Back Seat

The first time I had a glimpse into the other side of life in Burma, the side the government does not want foreigners to see, was in the back seat of a long black sedan. It was near the end of my first trip to the country.

A friend and I had spent several weeks visiting golden pagodas, intricately carved teak monasteries, spectacular waterfalls, and cool mountain retreats. Burma is a land of rich cultural and natural bounty, laced with an exoticism and spirituality that has intrigued foreigners for centuries. But we wanted to see the country behind the state-approved tourist sites, and were looking for encounters with local people whenever possible. Their ready smiles and shy curiosity charmed us at every turn.

Yet a distance remained. Many of our attempts to get closer to people – taking a rickety old train north from Rangoon to Mandalay, for instance, in hopes of striking up conversations with fellow passengers – were thwarted. In the case of the 480-kilometer train trip, the government booking agent assigned us to a first-class car whose only Burmese occupants were stony-faced military officers and their families. (My hopes were briefly lifted nine hours into the trip by a derailment on the line, which forced us and hundreds of Burmese passengers to disembark and carry our belongings along the tracks for several hundred meters to another train, but we were so closely observed by soldiers during the migration that there was no chance for conversation and the incident merely extended our long, hot journey by three hours.) In other instances when we managed to engage local people in conversation at cultural sites or in taxis, they were always kind, friendly and curious, but kept a careful distance from all but the most general topics.

One night we were in a little town in Upper Burma, enjoying spicy noodles in a local restaurant and chatting with the waitstaff, with whom we had become increasingly friendly during several repeat visits. Business in the restaurant was slow, and the young waiter lingered at our table. Always full of questions, we plied him for information on the town, local traditions, even the plants and trees we had seen during a bicycle trip through the lush surrounding countryside. He seemed pleased with our curiosity and knowledge about the country.

Near the end of the meal, we lamented the fact that we were leaving the following morning for Rangoon, and then heading back home. As so often happens in such forgotten corners of the world, the farther one gets off the beaten path, the less one wants to return to the city. Our desire to linger as long as possible in the far reaches of Upper Burma meant we were short on time and had to fly back to the capital. After listening quietly for a few minutes, our friend the waiter suggested that he could make arrangements to get us to the airport. I assumed he had a friend with a car who wanted to make some money, and we agreed.

The next morning, a large black sedan with tinted windows, a sight rarely seen outside Rangoon, let alone in such a small town, pulled up at our hotel. Out stepped the driver and a tall, distinguished-looking Burmese man in dark glasses. I noted that the man was wearing slacks instead of a *longyi*, the traditional ankle-length skirt worn by most men and women in Burma. The driver loaded our bags in the trunk under the other man's supervision, they returned to their places in the front seat of the car, and we settled in back for the trip the regional airport.

Riding in a Burmese car can be an unsettling experience for a foreigner since, under a system I have found nowhere else in the world, the steering wheel is located on the right side of the dashboard (as in Britain), but traffic moves on the right side of the road (as in the United States). The result is a situation where drivers sit hugging the outer shoulder of the pavement, and the act of passing another vehicle requires either a front-seat passenger to check for oncoming traffic, or nerves of steel. For this reason alone, I was happy to have the stranger sitting in front. We were racing down narrow country roads, regularly passing much slower-moving vehicles, with the driver blasting his horn to scatter chickens and swerving bicyclists at frequent intervals.

No one said a word for the first ten minutes of the trip. My friend and I gave each other searching looks. Who was the man in the passenger seat? Should we be concerned? His bearing suggested that he might be a government official, or perhaps a successful businessman. My curiosity got the better of me.

I leaned forward. 'Are you on the flight to Rangoon as well?' I asked.

'No, no,' he said. 'I wanted to accompany you to the airport.' His English was flawless. Now we were really curious.

My question was enough to start him talking. As the black sedan whizzed past verdant fields and ox-drawn carts rolling under a brilliant midday sun, U Hla Shwe told us about himself, and the situation his country was facing. Educated by Western missionaries (who taught generations of students until they were ejected from Burma by the government in the mid-1960s), U Hla Shwe grew up speaking English in school and had lived in Europe as a young man. When he returned to Burma more than twenty years ago, he had opened a business in this small town in Upper Burma, and had become quite successful over time.

So far, everything he had told us made me think he was a well-educated businessman who was eager to use his English with a couple of Westerners, particularly since travel out of the country has been more difficult for Burmese citizens in recent years. But why go to the trouble of taking us all the way to the airport in his private car? What he said next made us understand.

In 1990, U Hla Shwe was elected to serve in the national legislature as a representative of the country's fledgling opposition party, the National League for Democracy (NLD), which won a landslide victory in the first free election allowed by the military government since 1962. The results of the election were immediately annulled by the stunned government, and U Hla Shwe was thrown in jail along with hundreds of his party colleagues. We listened intently to his story from the back seat of the sedan, occasionally clutching the door handles as the driver sounded the horn and swerved to pass an ox cart.

In the little remaining time we had left en route to the airport, U Hla Shwe told us about things that are carefully hidden from the view of foreign visitors to Burma. 'People here are living in fear,' he said, 'the world needs to know that.'

He spoke of a country that seemed completely removed from the images of Buddhist harmony we had absorbed over the past couple of weeks. The Burma he described was a land of military controls, an intelligence network designed to make neighbor suspect neighbor, thousands of refugees from minority tribes driven into camps across the Thai border, and a government that was wringing money from the system while the people struggled to make ends meet amid surging inflation. It was also, he said, a country that felt cut off from the world.

'People here are desperate for information,' he said. 'Bring newspapers and magazines if you come again. People need to know what's happening outside of Burma. And they need to know the world has not forgotten them.'

All too soon, we pulled up in front of the regional airport. U Hla Shwe urged us to make time in Rangoon to see Aung San Suu Kyi, the opposition leader and Nobel Peace Prize winner who was giving speeches every weekend in front of her home at the time, although she was living under virtual house arrest. Then he wished us well, and said goodbye.

U Hla Shwe stayed seated behind the tinted windows as we climbed out of his car and hoisted the bags over our shoulders. It had been a brief, but impressionable, encounter that made me realize we had only scratched the surface of this country. I knew I would be back.

Chapter 2

The Lady

The day after our back-seat encounter with U Hla Shwe, we went to see Aung San Suu Kyi speak in a pouring rain. Several hundred people, predominantly Burmese with a handful of curious foreigners sprinkled among them, were seated or standing along Rangoon's leafy University Avenue in front of a high wall ringing the opposition leader's house. It was a well-tended, upper-class neighborhood near Inya Lake, and seemed an unlikely setting for such a mass gathering. Many people brought pieces of plastic to sit on, but others just crouched in muddy puddles on the narrow strip of land between the street and the wall. A few people had fashioned hats out of plastic bags, and there were some umbrellas at the back of the crowd, but most of them sat quietly with wet hair plastered on their heads as the rain poured down their faces. It was an orderly, almost reverential gathering.

The woman they had come to see stood on a raised platform behind the high wall. She was slender, fine-boned and beautifully dressed in a bright green tunic and patterned *longyi*, with a wide-brimmed straw hat to keep the rain out of her face. A small cluster of white flowers in her hair was just visible under the hat. She looked amazingly fresh compared with the rest of us, and appeared to be much younger than a woman in her fifties. The two burly young men who stood alongside her behind the wall and a dozen other aides who formed a ring in front of her on the ground below were so soaked that their thin white shirts were transparent, stuck to their chests. In contrast to the stony-faced young men, The Lady (as she is known among the people) was beaming.

Aung San Suu Kyi – the daughter of slain independence leader Aung San, the head of the outlawed National League for Democracy, winner of the 1990 national election, and recipient of the Nobel Peace Prize – spoke for an hour that day on the power of nonviolent resistance. She drew heavily on examples of successful movements in other countries, and focused particularly on the 'velvet revolution' in the former Czechoslovakia (Vaclav Havel, a one-time dissident who became the Czechoslovak president, had nominated her for the Nobel Peace Prize several years earlier.) Her tone was passionate at times, but generally, she had the air of a Sunday school teacher who was trying to move her pupils with moral suasion.

The crowd listened intently. A steady stream of traffic, with gawkers hanging out the windows of pickup trucks that are a popular form of public transport in Rangoon, passed slowly behind us on University

Avenue. We had been told that these gatherings were videotaped by the Burmese government, and sure enough, we spotted video cameras on a hill across the road. No one around us seemed to pay the least bit of attention to them. They were too absorbed by The Lady.

In deference to the few foreigners in the crowd, Aung San Suu Kyi switched from Burmese to English for the final ten minutes of her speech. In the very proper English accent she honed during years living in Britain prior to returning to Burma in 1988, she recapped the message she had shared that day with her Burmese followers. 'Let us demonstrate our desire through peaceful and disciplined means,' she urged the crowd. In closing, she appealed to the foreigners present to tell the world about Burma's plight.

'I come here every weekend I am able to,' said a middle-aged Burmese man standing next to me in the rain. 'We do not know how long it will last. Daw Suu gives us inspiration.' There was an unspoken acknowledgement in his words that these weekly mass gatherings, which began after Aung San Suu Kyi was released from six years of house arrest in 1995, were flirting with the limits of government tolerance. Sure enough, the gatherings were banned by the junta in late 1996, only a few months after our visit, when pro-democracy demonstrations briefly flared again on the nation's university campuses. The Lady was apparently considered too potent a symbol to be allowed in front of a crowd.

Aung San Suu Kyi was only two years old when her father, General Aung San, a national hero who led Burma's struggle for independence from Britain and against the Japanese occupation, was assassinated in July 1947. The assassination occurred only a few months before Britain formally transferred power to Burma, a handover that Aung San had negotiated. A jealous political rival masterminded the killing.

Aung San Suu Kyi later left Burma with her mother and lived in India for a number of years. She was educated in New Delhi and at Oxford University, and then worked for the United Nations in New York and Bhutan. Married to a British academic, she made her home in Oxford, England, and had two sons. Although she had only the faintest memories of her father, Aung San Suu Kyi (who added his name to the front of her own) was an avid student of Aung San's life and ideas. She published a biography of his life in 1984. 'When I honor my father, I honor all those who stand for political integrity in Burma,' she wrote. From abroad, she also strove to maintain her contact with Burma, and was preparing to write a doctoral thesis on Burmese literature for London University when she unexpectedly returned to Rangoon in 1988.

The event that brought Aung San Suu Kyi back to Burma in the spring of 1988 was not the fledgling democracy movement, but rather her mother's poor health. Daw Khin Kyi suffered a severe stroke in March 1988, and her daughter immediately returned to Rangoon to care for her. By the time Daw Khin Kyi died in late December 1988, Burma had experienced nine of the most tumultuous months in the country's history. A tide of revolt, led first by university students and then picked up by people from all walks of life, had swept the country. The military government, temporarily thrown into disarray, responded with increasing use of force.

As the democracy movement gathered steam through the summer and fall of 1988, Aung San Suu Kyi had been swept to the core of the escalating conflict. Her family home on the shores of Inya Lake became a center for political discussion and debate. Her first public address was made in front of Rangoon Hospital in August 1988, and two days later she addressed a mass rally in front of Shwedagon Pagoda, the holiest Buddhist site in the country and a symbolically charged venue for such an event.

Even at that early stage in the movement, she sensed the importance of taking the pro-democracy message beyond Burma's borders. 'This public rally is aimed at informing the whole world of the will of the people,' she had proclaimed at the outset of the Shwedagon speech. Over the next eleven months, until she was placed under house arrest, she gave approximately one thousand public addresses to supporters all over the country.

Eventually, it was too much for the military government. They placed her under house arrest in July 1989, and did not release her until mid-1995. Despite this attempt to silence Aung San Suu Kyi and the opposition movement she headed, the government inexplicably allowed a nationwide election to be held in May 1990. The National League for Democracy, the party that Aung San Suu Kyi had founded, won by a landslide with more than 80 percent of the vote. The results were immediately annulled by the junta and hundreds of party members were thrown in jail, many for several years. But the people's message was undeniable.

Listening to Aung San Suu Kyi speak on that rainy Saturday in 1996, I recognized that this slight, elegant woman was still the single individual with the greatest power to transform Burma. She is one of the few people inside the country who has repeatedly and publicly stood up to the generals, and despite everything they have done to her, she has not shown signs of backing down. Much of her power, of course, has stemmed from her legacy as the daughter of a national hero. But through her words and actions, she had demonstrated a genuine concern for the people of Burma, and they had responded with an overwhelming display of support.

Her support continues to this day. On each of my visits to Burma, many people that I had a chance to speak with quietly for more than a few minutes – ranging from taxi drivers to people I met at the pagodas – would quietly invoke Aung San Suu Kyi's name. It was always uttered in hushed tones, and was usually dropped unexpectedly in the middle of conversations about completely unrelated topics. They would suddenly ask:

'Do you know of Aung San Suu Kyi?' or

'Have you seen The Lady?'

A simple nod of recognition from me was enough to make their faces light up, as if we shared an unspoken bond. Then, they would quickly return to the prior, safer topic of discussion. Generally, the conversation ended soon afterward, before we attracted too much attention. It seemed to be enough for them to know that people outside Burma were aware of the struggle underway there.

Despite the general population's adoration of Aung San Suu Kyi, there is a small but growing group of people in Rangoon who have criticized the opposition leader for being too stubborn and uncompromising with the military regime. She has backed herself into a corner, they say, providing no room to maneuver with the government.

There have been recent signs that the opposition party is fraying at the edges. In early 1999, a group of NLD members elected to parliament in 1990 held a government-sanctioned press conference to urge the party to start a dialogue with the junta. Aung San Suu Kyi immediately dismissed them as 'collaborators' with the military regime.

To date, no clear successor to Aung San Suu Kyi has emerged within the opposition party ranks. Members of several minority ethnic groups in Burma, who are waging their own struggles for autonomy, told me that she is the only NLD official they trust, because they believe she shares her father's willingness to deal fairly with the minority groups. They voiced concerns about other NLD leaders, such as ex-General Tin Oo, who was chief-of-staff and minister of defense when minority insurgents were active in the mid-1970s. The wariness about other top NLD officers was voiced by some Burmans as well.

'The NLD is suffering from an image problem,' a Rangoon-based writer told me in mid-1999. 'Part of the problem is with the few people surrounding Aung San Suu Kyi. They're former military officers, and many people do not trust them. People call them "the men in pants", because they have worn military uniforms for so long.'

Despite the few voices who question some of the NLD leadership, Aung San Suu Kyi remains firmly in control of the opposition. One of her important roles has been as a mobilizer of international support for the cause of Burmese democracy and human rights. There are many people who fear that without her, international pressure on Burma – and prospects for change – would dwindle.

Recognizing the influence that Aung San Suu Kyi continues to wield both inside and outside Burma, the government has kept the pressure on her since her release from house arrest in 1995. Her movements are still tightly monitored and restricted. Visitors to her compound in Rangoon are frequently subject to harassment. Foreign journalists who meet with her are often taken straight to the airport afterward, with the authorities pausing only long enough to search them and cull through their luggage.

In late 1998, the government's standoff with the opposition grew more aggressive. Hundreds of NLD officials and members were arrested and held in government 'guest houses' for months. By mid-1999, an estimated 26,000 NLD members and eighteen elected members of parliament had been coaxed into 'resigning' from the party since the latest government crackdown had begun. More than fifty party offices had been closed. During Burma's National Day celebrations in February 1999, one of the nation's top generals made a speech calling for the opposition to be 'annihilated'. At the time, Aung San Suu Kyi and her supporters were distributing rice to the poor in Rangoon.

⚬⚬⚬

The most personal attempt by the government to break Aung San Suu Kyi's spirit, however, surrounded her husband's death in the spring of 1999. Dr Michael Aris, a respected professor of Tibetan studies at Oxford University, had not been granted a visa to visit his wife in Burma for more than two years. When Dr Aris was diagnosed with cancer at age fifty-two, he immediately intensified efforts to visit his wife. She did not want to leave Burma to visit him for fear she would be barred from returning. As the seriousness of his illness became known, governments from around the world, as well as the United Nations Secretary General, appealed to the Burmese authorities to issue a visa to Dr Aris on humanitarian grounds. The authorities refused all the requests, and Dr Aris died at a London hospital on 27 March 1999, his fifty-third birthday, without seeing his wife again. The incident prompted a wave of scorn and outrage that was directed at the Burmese authorities from individuals and governments around the world.

I saw Aung San Suu Kyi again only weeks after her husband's death. It was a scorching hot day in Rangoon when I made a visit to NLD party headquarters. As I climbed out of a taxi in front of the building, which was adorned with flags defiantly flapping in the wind, I noticed the military intelligence officers seated in a tea shop directly across the street, observing and recording the movements of people in and out of the NLD office.

Stepping from the bright sunlight into the dimly lit building, I was surprised to see at least one hundred people crowding the large meeting room. They sat on wooden benches and stood chatting in small clusters underneath a giant mural of Aung San Suu Kyi, which was painted on the balcony above us.

It was mostly a young crowd, but people of all ages were there. Several elderly ladies were checking in people at a table near the front door, and an old man with a cane wobbled across the stifling room. As the only Westerner in the crowd, I was accorded special treatment and immediately offered a chair next to a monk. Seeing the perspiration running down my face, a young man wearing an NLD pin brought me a cold bottle of soda and handed me a paper fan. A collage on the wall beside me featured old photographs and currency notes featuring General Aung San, the opposition leader's father.

Despite all the official attempts to discourage her, Aung San Suu Kyi still met the public at NLD headquarters twice a week. These were open sessions, led by the senior party leaders, who took turns addressing the crowd. Their speeches were followed by a question-and-answer session.

When Aung San Suu Kyi finally made her appearance on that day, the buzz in the room immediately stopped. People who had dozed through speeches by the other NLD leaders were suddenly awake and attentive. The Lady wore a light brown tunic, a dark *longyi*, and was missing the flowers in her hair that had become a trademark. She looked much more tired than when I had seen her in the past, but still appeared cooler and more composed than most of us in the sauna-like conditions.

She spent the next half-hour addressing the attentive crowd on issues of democracy, equality and human rights, holding to the themes that had been a constant during the struggle she had led for eleven years. Her voice was strong and confident. When she was finished, she remained for another hour answering questions from individual citizens who shared their concerns about the twin burdens of government repression and growing economic hardship.

I knew that the following day, Aung San Suu Kyi would be hosting hundreds of monks and other dignitaries at her home to mark the one-month anniversary of her husband's death.

She undoubtedly had numerous arrangements to finalize before receiving such a large group of guests.

But for the time being, her attention was focused only on the people.

Chapter 3

'Students' Forever

Delving deeper into the story of Burma's people, I became in-trigued with the fate of the university students who had fueled the pro-democracy movement of 1988-89. They had started demonstrating in the streets of Rangoon months before Aung San Suu Kyi got formally involved in the movement or gave her first public address.

Whenever I met Burmese men and women in their late twenties and early thirties on my visits to the country, I found myself wondering what they had been doing in the late 1980s. Much as the Chinese democracy movement that culminated at Tiananmen Square in June 1989 was a defining period in the lives of thousands of young Chinese, so the democracy movement in Rangoon and other cities throughout 1988-89 was a defining period in the lives of thousands of Burmese students. The estimated 3,000 deaths during Burma's democracy movement were significantly higher than the death toll at Tiananmen Square.

But CNN did not broadcast live from Rangoon. Indeed, months of dramatic street demonstrations in the Burmese capital went largely unrecognized by the rest of the world. During one three-day period in September 1988, an estimated one thousand people were killed. Many of them were university students and Buddhist monks. Photographers who captured the events on film were thrown in jail and ordered to burn their pictures. Protests and rallies continued into the following year, until Aung San Suu Kyi was placed under house arrest. It was not until the opposition leader was awarded the Nobel Peace Prize in 1991 that much of the world became aware of Burma at all.

A decade later, I wondered what had become of the student leaders who rose up against the military government, only to see thousands of their fellow protestors gunned down by in the streets of Rangoon? In a country where less than one-third of children complete primary school, those who were admitted to university were truly the best and the brightest of their generation.

Eventually, I met with former student leaders both inside and outside of Burma. I learned that, as with many highly politicized groups, this one too had fragmented in the decade since the democracy movement swept the country. The most radical of the students (among those that survived) were either still in jail in Burma, had fled the country, or had lived for years in the jungle along the Thai-Burmese border, where they took refuge in camps and waged armed rebellion against the government alongside fighters from ethnic minority tribes.

A large group of former Burmese students today lives in Bangkok, which remains the region's hub for Burma-watching and activism. Others who got out of the country eventually settled in the United States, Australia, Japan, and other countries throughout the Asia-Pacific region. Today, these overseas Burmese continue the struggle (in the form of regular news releases about abuses in the country, letter-writing campaigns, etc.) through involvement with organizations like the All Burma Students' Democratic Front. Several of the overseas dissident organizations have been plagued with infighting and recriminations.

So who were these former student leaders who continued to wage the struggle against Burma's military government from abroad? I found several of them who were willing to share their stories with me. Tin Hlaing was one such young man whose radical views were formed during the street protests of 1988, and hardened during two and a half years of guerrilla warfare in the jungle. Today he is a PhD candidate in the United States, but he vows that he will return to Burma someday.

He looked like just another graduate student on the American university campus. His black hair was slightly disheveled, and he wore a bright purple sweatshirt, faded jeans and Timberland boots. He looked me in the eye, gave me a firm handshake, and used his free hand to push up a pair of wire-rimmed glasses on his nose. At thirty-three, he still had an impish grin. But when he began to tell his story, it was clear that this young man was far from the typical graduate student at a US university. Once he started remembering, the events came back in vivid detail.

Tin Hlaing's roots were fairly ordinary. He was born into a humble Buddhist family in a village in Lower Burma. (The term dates from the nineteenth century; Britain annexed the 'lower', or southern, part of central Burma in 1852 and the 'upper', or northern, part of the country in 1886, although coastal regions were annexed as early as 1826.) Tin Hlaing's parents were peasants who, over time, had to sell off their land to earn money for their family. His mother was also an accomplished potter. Tin Hlaing was the youngest of six children, one of two boys in the family. He recalled his older brother's tragic death at an early age as his 'first trauma in life'.

Tin Hlaing was an exceptional student in high school, where he earned honors in all subjects. At age seventeen, he left his home village and began his university studies at a regional college. In 1981 he was poised to enter the country's prestigious Institute of Medicine when his father died unexpectedly.

'I was devastated and quit school,' Tin Hlaing told me. 'Because of the stress, I got a stomach ulcer, which had to be treated for two years.' During the time he was away from classes, the regional college system was reformed. When he was ready to return to school, he found himself out of step with the new system's regulations.

'I was in limbo, and the educational authorities said I could not join the medical college,' Tin Hlaing said. Instead, he was admitted to Rangoon University, the nation's largest institution of higher education. Abandoning his plans to go into medicine, Tin Hlaing chose to study English literature and linguistics, because 'teaching English is not a bad career in Burma'.

In 1988, Tin Hlaing was a second-year graduate student at Rangoon University and was an active member of the All Burma Federation of Students' Unions, an umbrella organization of all student unions. It was a role that put him close to the center of events as the pro-democracy movement began to take shape.

The movement had formed against a backdrop of economic and social tension. In September 1987, without warning, the Burmese government suddenly devalued the three highest denomination banknotes in the country, and took them out of circulation. Overnight, the move wiped out the entire savings of many Burmese families. In addition, the action had an inflationary effect on prices, as people rushed to purchase tangible goods with the little currency they had left. The population was charged with anger and frustration. The tension, combined with years of repression and abuse at the hands of the military government, gave birth to a fledgling democracy movement on the campus of Rangoon University.

In the early months, the student movement was far from organized. In March 1988, Tin Hlaing recalled, he was involved in a peaceful student protest on the Rangoon University campus that prompted the government to respond with force. 'When riot police stormed the campus, I, like others, fled as the police charged ahead with batons and tear gas,' he told me. 'I remember I jumped over a fence, crossed the road, and ran into the residential neighborhood nearby. But some of the riot police chased us, so I and a few students ran to a house that happened to be the home of a diplomat from an East European country. The Communist official was highly sympathetic, and hid us in his house until it got dark. Then, we slipped out one by one and took the bus home. Those who did not escape were beaten seriously, either to death or unconscious, then packed into paddy wagons and whisked to Insein jail' outside of Rangoon.

Later the same week, the movement gathered momentum when thousands of local citizens joined the students in a massive rally in downtown Rangoon. According to Tin Hlaing, the student leaders had been 'desperate and distressed' at the time due to a heavy police presence on the university campus and a further crackdown on peaceful student protestors the day before.

'It looked like our protests had met a hopeless end,' he said. In a bold move, a few of his close friends suddenly decided to act on a plan they had been discussing: they hijacked two Toyota pickup trucks that carried paying passengers along a route near the university campus, 'asked the passengers to get out, put a flag up and drove'.

As the hijacked trucks headed toward downtown around mid-afternoon, the students inside began to shout that 'a huge column of students' was marching toward downtown, and encouraged office workers crowding the streets to join them. The students also shouted pro-democracy and anti-government slogans. Of course, Tin Hlaing noted, it was all a bluff. There was no column of students.

The ploy was effective, and a crowd began to gather in the streets, but not all the instigators escaped. One of the two hijacked pickup trucks was chased by military intelligence, and all the students in it were arrested. Students in the other truck eventually abandoned it downtown and escaped into the crowd, waving their flags as they ran. The crowd behind them grew, fueled by thousands of Muslims who came pouring out of Rangoon's downtown mosques after their Friday prayers just as the rally gathered momentum.

'The crowd grew bigger and speeches began,' Tin Hlaing recalled. People grew angry. What was intended as a peaceful protest started to turn violent. Government cars were set on fire in front of government buildings, government-owned buses were overturned, and stones were thrown at riot police who arrived on the scene.

'When I reached downtown, the rally was in full swing and cars were burning,' Tin Hlaing said. 'More and more riot police came, backed by army units. Armored carriers also rolled in. People started storming into government buildings.... Finally, riot police overwhelmed people with tear gas and batons. Hundreds were dead, but their bodies were quickly snatched up and dumped into trucks by police. We know that later their bodies were secretly burned at Kyandaw Cemetery.... Hundreds of people were packed into paddy wagons.'

In one of the most tragic single incidents of the movement, forty-one people died when they were packed into a paddy wagon and suffocated in the heat. The event was so stunning that even Ne Win, the government strongman, issued a public apology. A number of observers have suggested that the extent of police brutality in Rangoon during March 1988 helped the democracy movement take root among the broader population.

Three of Tin Hlaing's friends were involved in starting the March rally, he said. He has stayed in contact with two of them, one of whom is still in jail.

For Tin Hlaing, the violence of March 1988 began to harden his views against the military. Several months later, in June, he was involved in another protest march that went from Medical College Number One to downtown Rangoon. Riot police were called in and blocked the road, he recalled. After an hour of confrontation with the unarmed protestors, the police started to charge.

'I remember a couple of young high school kids in the front were severely beaten and one collapsed and died,' he said. 'Seeing this savage scene, onlookers picked up anything they could find nearby to throw at the police.' People brought out slingshots, which were popular at the time, and some picked up nuts and bolts from auto parts shops in the neighborhood to shoot at the police. A number of government troops were killed. 'Some students took the dead body of the young student, propped it on the hood of a pickup truck and drove it all around in the residential neighborhoods of Hlaing township,' he said. 'People were so angry, they destroyed government buildings.'

I wondered how Tin Hlaing had escaped injury or capture on so many occasions during the tumultuous months of 1988. 'My friends called me "Mr Lucky" because I was able to run away unscathed in the March and June incidents,' he said. 'But I should have been killed, I swear, in the protest on 19 September 1988, one day after the coup.'

In September 1988, after a month of relative openness under the short-lived government of Maung Maung, the government of Burma was dissolved and replaced by a military council called the State Law and Order Restoration Council. The event was not really a coup at all, but rather a move by the military to sweep aside its civilian figurehead and take direct control of the government that it had managed from behind the scenes all along. A curfew was imposed and demonstrations were banned, as were assemblies of more than four people.

Tin Hlaing recalled that on 19 September, the day after the military action, marchers filled the streets of Rangoon. Thousands of protestors were on the street in front of the US Embassy. Several blocks away, Tin Hlaing was among a column of protestors that was marching past the Government Secretariat, an ominous-looking structure, when troops started firing on them.

'I saw a couple of students and one college teacher mowed down by bullets,' he told me. 'Our instinct was to duck down. There were also snipers on the tops of buildings nearby. As students tried to run away, the snipers shot them. I did the same thing, but the bullets missed me. Perhaps they missed me because so many students were running in different directions at the same moment. I escaped again.' A similar scene of carnage was unfolding around the US Embassy on the same day.

The nineteenth of September was a turning point for Tin Hlaing. 'After the coup, we students were divided,' he said. 'One group thought we should remain in the cities, monitor the situation and engage in political activities since the new military council set up by the old guard promised elections. The other group, including myself, was so radicalized by the killings that there was no way left but armed resistance. So I left for the jungle.'

He and a group of other student leaders took a bus to the southeastern city of Moulmein, in the thin strip of Burma that snakes south between the sea and Thailand. From there, they trekked east through mountainous jungle for days, heading toward the Thai border. The group was joined by several high school students from Moulmein. 'At the time, hundreds of groups like mine were leaving Burma for the jungle,' he said. An estimated 10,000 students left for the border areas after the crackdown on the pro-democracy movement.

Tin Hlaing spent the next two and a half years living in the jungle among ethnic guerrilla fighters, waging an armed struggle against Burmese government forces. First, he stayed at a large student camp called Theybawbo in an area controlled by resistance fighters of the Karen ethnic group. Almost a year later, he moved to a Mon-controlled area to join a student group led by the son of the ex-Prime Minister U Nu. Internal disagreements among the various student groups were common, and many of the students eventually returned home to their families.

'I believed armed resistance was necessary,' Tin Hlaing said. 'We were trained and engaged in battles along with the ethnic resistance fighters. I was actually sent to special training for urban guerrilla tactics.' He declined to elaborate on what such tactics entailed.

'Life was terrible' in the camps, he said. 'The food was bad. Malaria, hepatitis and other diseases were killing student guerrillas faster than the battles were. Only rice and fish paste were available. Meat was a luxury, and we got to eat meat only once in two months. Vegetables were not available. Foodstuffs were either imported from the Thai side of the border, or bought from villagers.'

Tin Hlaing was stricken with malaria not once, but twice. After the second attack, he decided he had to leave the Burmese jungle for Thailand, since 'nobody survived the third attack' of malaria.

So Tin Hlaing walked to the border and crossed into Thailand. At the time, Burmese students were being recognized by the United Nations

High Commission for Refugees (UNHCR) as asylum-seekers. Unlike many other Burmese who had fled across the border, the students were not confined to refugee camps. Through a program supported by Senator Daniel Patrick Moynihan, Tin Hlaing was eventually sponsored to go to the United States by the US Information Agency and the US State Department. He enrolled at an American university, and began graduate studies in political science.

For those he left behind in Burma, life remains difficult. 'My friends were given fifteen-year sentences as recently as last March,' he told me in late 1998. 'This was the second time they were jailed. The first time, the sentences were much shorter. My family is harassed by the secret police and other authorities, and my close relatives cannot get passports because of me.'

Tin Hlaing said he remains in close contact with the exiled dissident community. His ambition is to be 'one of those who will rebuild Burma'. He has no doubt that he will go back one day. But he expressed intense frustration at the current situation in the country.

'The situation is highly volatile,' he said. 'I cannot predict what will happen, but I believe the prospects for change are really high. Others might not agree with me, but the truth is that the people want change. They expressed that, and they keep on expressing that, though they are muffled by the force of guns. That's the important thing: people.'

While Tin Hlaing has continued the struggle for democracy from his campus in the United States, Sammy is a contemporary who has never left the jungles along the Thai-Burmese border. Now thirty-four years old, this 'student' has moved from camp to camp more than twenty times since leaving his home in Burma in 1988 to join fellow students fighting the military regime. He became a brigade commander of the student forces, and spent more than a decade waging armed resistance in the jungle.

I met Sammy over dinner one night in a northern Thai town where he had traveled by bus from his camp along the Burmese border, eluding several checkpoints en route. If he had been detected by the Thai authorities on the way to our meeting, he said nonchalantly, he would have been put in jail for a minimum of twenty-eight days and then shipped back to the border. It had happened to him numerous times before, he noted, ticking off the names of Thai cities where he had been arrested.

Fortunately there were no problems on this occasion. Sammy was an articulate, handsome man of Indian descent who wore blue jeans and a sport shirt with a gold pen clipped to the pocket. He had a brilliant white smile that frequently lit up his dark-skinned face. We met for dinner on a balmy evening at a quiet riverside cafe. As an ensemble played traditional Thai music in the background, he smoked and drank beer and talked about life as a revolutionary. He certainly did not *look* like someone who had been a brigade commander in the jungle for a decade, narrowly escaping death on several occasions, living on his wits and the little food that could be scavenged in the wild. I had expected to meet someone more ragged-looking, someone less polished. But Sammy had plenty of stories to tell.

'In the beginning, more than 10,000 Burmese students fled to the border regions' after the military cracked down on pro-democracy demonstrators in 1988-89, he told me. 'More than half of them went home within three months. The food was bad and conditions were tough. Malaria was our number one enemy at that time. Over time, many students crossed into Thailand and applied for asylum with the UNHCR. By the end of 1990, about 3,000 students remained along the Thai-Burmese border.'

Labels are important to past and present members of this group. They still call themselves 'students', although most are in their thirties now and have not been inside a classroom for more than a decade. Those of them that crossed into Thailand seeking asylum, and those like Sammy, who often stays at a camp just inside the Thai border that is within a few meters of a refugee camp, also make a point to distinguish themselves from the hundreds of thousands of their countrymen who have fled to Thailand seeking permanent refuge from fighting and abuse in Burma. (The head of a relief organization in northern Thailand recalled that in 1988 and 1989, the town of Mae Sot was overflowing with Burmese students who insisted they be called 'revolutionaries', not 'refugees'.)

The student fighters were armed by various ethnic resistance groups who were also fighting Burma's military government. Chinese rifles and American rifles from the Vietnam war-era were commonly used. The students also had access to HK-33 automatic assault rifles, which Sammy said were 'easy to buy'.

I asked about the use of force by formerly peaceful students. 'For the first few years, we were motivated purely by revenge,' Sammy said. 'No one questioned the use of armed resistance after seeing the military use such violence with the pro-democracy demonstrators. We believed that in six months to three years, five years at the most, we would overthrow the military government and return home.' The result had seemed like such a certainty to them at the time.

But the years stretched on, the Burmese army continued to grow in size and strength, and a war of attrition took its toll on the student fighters in the jungle. Life was difficult and often dangerous. 'I've had bullets within two inches of my head, but so far, I've never been injured,' Sammy said. As a brigade commander, he was generally farther back from the front lines than other students.

Each time the student fighters moved to a new location in the jungle, they would build little huts using thatch and bamboo. They had only knives to work with, and used no nails. Meals consisted mainly of rice, salt, and vegetables, but the students tried to supplement their diets by hunting when there was a lull in the fighting.

'The jungle is our supermarket,' Sammy declared. 'We try to find deer, birds, or snakes when we have the chance. Sometimes we will drop a grenade in a stream to kill the fish, and dry them. We're very happy when we get wild pigs.' It is forbidden to kill tigers, elephants, peacocks and bear, all of which still roam the mountainous regions of Burma, he noted.

Today, there are five to six hundred student revolutionaries left along the Thai border, Sammy estimated, with another two hundred of them scattered along Burma's borders with China and India. Most have been pushed up against the borders as a result of offensives in recent years by the Burmese army and the Democratic Karen Buddhist Army (DKBA), a splinter group of ethnic Karen fighters that has sided with the military junta. As a result of the increased pressure, Sammy and his fellow students are forced to spend more of their time at camps inside Thailand now, and take shorter trips into Burma.

'When we go inside Burma now, we move every day and we don't build huts,' he said. 'If it is clear, we will sometimes stay in villages. But some villagers have been attacked and tortured for sheltering us, so we need to be very cautious.'

Even life on the Thai side of the border can be risky. Sammy recounted an incident in 1997 when his student camp in Thailand, which was ten meters from a refugee camp, was attacked by DKBA forces. Two people were killed and nine wounded. In another incident, a Burmese military group crossed the Thai border to arrest him in the middle of the night. 'When they got near the camp, a dog started barking and an inexperienced young soldier shot it,' he said. 'That alerted some of the refugees who were living around us, and they chased the soldiers away. I heard the shots but thought I was dreaming. I didn't hear the full story until the next morning.'

In recent years, Sammy served as a central committee member of the All Burma Students' Democratic Front. The ABSDF is a leading student organization involved in the struggle for democracy in Burma, although it is based outside the country. Two years ago, the group made a decision to change its tactics.

'We've decided to stop the armed struggle, and to pursue non-violent means,' Sammy told me. 'We don't have enough manpower and facilities left to keep up the fight. The Burmese army is getting rid of us one by one.' He declined to say how many students had been killed in battle, but estimated that 40 percent of ABSDF members had been injured. 'Besides,' he added, 'the Burmese government is most afraid of political works and a movement by the people. So our committee decided to change its policy. Not everyone agreed, but that was the decision.'

I asked Sammy what made him continue the struggle that so many others had abandoned. 'It's a difficult question,' he admitted. 'Those of us who have stayed are like brothers and sisters in the jungle. We are very close. We are all committed to the cause.'

Had he ever been tempted to leave, I persisted? 'I could go abroad and get democracy for myself,' he said. 'But that would not bring democracy for the people. My place is here.'

It is much harder to find members of the 'student' generation in the heartland of Burma who are willing, or able, to talk. Among the former student leaders who remain in the country, many are behind bars. Those who are not in prison tend to keep low profiles. (In January 1999, a Bangkok-based exile group reported that two hundred Burmese students were sentenced to long prison terms – sentences of fifty-two, thirty-eight, twenty-three and twenty-one years were reportedly given to four of the activists – for demanding that the national parliament elected in 1990 be convened.)

Most of the former student activists who live inside Burma have moved on with their lives. Many are married now, with families and steady jobs. Yet they remain aware that their past activities make them subject to closer scrutiny by the government's vast intelligence network than most average Burmese citizens.

If Sammy and Tin Hlaing were near one end of the spectrum in terms of their activism more than a decade after the democracy movement, Mya Nyunt was near the other end of the spectrum. I first encountered him standing behind the counter of his business – a small hotel/restaurant complex in Upper Burma – with a broad grin on his chubby face and gold rings on his fingers. He hardly looked like a one-time political activist. As a successful businessman in his early thirties, he had a stocky build that made him look more like a contented Buddha.

I had expected something else, perhaps someone more strident or idealistic. But a mutual friend has assured me that ten years earlier Mya Nyunt was in the thick of the demonstrations that shook this country to its core. It was one of the many lessons I was to learn about Burma: appearances can be deceiving.

I sat down with him over tea one morning in a quiet corner of the hotel restaurant. He was cautious at first, but he warmed up a bit with time. A thoughtful man with a ready smile, he was ready to discuss his family and business interests, but seemed uncertain whether to tell me about the details of his student days. Slowly, we worked backward.

As a student at Rangoon University, Mya Nyunt was caught up in the excitement of the democracy movement that built on campus in 1988-89. Close to graduation, he had to put his plans on hold when the government shut the universities in August 1988, a tactic used repeatedly in recent decades. Although he was not involved with organizing the early demonstrations in Rangoon that spring and summer of 1988, the university shutdown gave Mya Nyunt and many other students an incentive to get involved in political organizing. As a national opposition movement took shape, he was assigned to organize political activities in his hometown in Upper Burma.

'We only wanted democracy, a change in the government,' Mya Nyunt said, with some hesitation. (Unlike dissidents now living outside the country who offered detailed descriptions of the democracy protests and the government crackdown, Mya Nyunt preferred to speak in generalities.)

When the government crackdown on student organizers finally occurred, Mya Nyunt was exceptionally lucky. Although he was arrested, he was held behind bars for only four days. The conditions were cramped and chaotic, he recalled, with more than forty students jammed in a cell meant for six people, but he managed to leave prison without suffering harm.

Many of his friends were not so fortunate. Several of them were tortured. One of the tortured men, whose extended prison stay included four months in solitary confinement, stopped by Mya Nyunt's home one night while I was there. When our conversation turned to his days in prison, he showed me the backs of his legs. I saw scars where his Achilles tendons had been cut by soldiers who he described as 'frightened young country boys'. He still suffers the psychological effects of his time in solitary confinement.

What is striking in conversations today with Mya Nyunt, and many others like him, is the extent to which many of these young men and women who led the boldest popular uprising in Burma's tumultuous recent history have moved on with their lives. After all, in a country where the military junta controls all the strings, there is virtually no outlet for an organized opposition. Indeed, the government rounded up hundreds of NLD members in 1998, held them at state-run 'guesthouses' and pressured them to resign from the party.

Throughout my travels in Burma, I encountered young men and women in their late twenties and early thirties who once marched in the streets and openly called for democracy. In the decade since then, the government has been virtually unchanged – aside from a name change from SLORC to SPDC in 1997 – and the Burmese people have suffered worsening economic straits. (In mid-1999, inflation was running at a 50 percent annual rate, according to analysts, and the country's currency was severely weakened. The *kyat* was trading at 350 to the U.S. dollar on the black market, despite an official exchange rate of 6 kyat to the dollar.) Yet the movement's former grassroots organizers – those inside the country, that is – have largely remained quiet. It appears to be a very practical matter of survival.

Mya Nyunt's friends reflected the paths that many of their fellow classmates had taken. 'Most of them are in business – real estate, tourism, that kind of thing – or they are traders,' he said. A number of them had left the country for Japan, Singapore or Malaysia, where job opportunities seemed more promising. Mya Nyunt and his friends exemplify a generation that has taken a pragmatic approach to the turmoil and continued repression in his country. 'Life goes on,' he said.

But then Mya Nyunt was pragmatic even as a younger man. When the university in Rangoon was closed due to demonstrations in 1988, he was studying geology. In an effort to keep advancing his education, after the shutdown he split his time between political organizing and visits to the Bogyoke Aung San and Mogok Street markets in Rangoon, watching gem dealers at work and asking questions.

His time at the gem markets would pave the way for his later career. The son of goldsmiths, he returned to his hometown after he was finally able to finish university, and worked in the family business for a year. At that point, he set off with a friend to make his fortune at the famed northern gem mines in Mogok and Maungshwe. Mogok rubies are reputed to be the purest in Burma and are known around the world.

When they eventually tired of life in the mines, Mya Nyunt and his friend moved on to jobs in a regional gem market, where they became gem dealers. Thousands of stones change hands each day in the market, which is merely a collection of crude wooden tables and benches. Traders clustered around piles of purplish raw rubies with magnifying glasses and weights, haggling over prices.

In a country where the average monthly wage is about 10,000 kyat (US$28 at the 1999 black market rate), gem dealers earn a minimum of 1,000 kyat a day and some earn more than 10,000 kyat a day. Not only did Mya Nyunt earn a substantial sum of money in his three years at the gem market, he also met his wife there. As a teenager, she worked in her family's gem brokering business and frequently came to the market, where she and Mya Nyunt met. They married when she finished the tenth standard in school, at age eighteen. Mya Nyunt was twenty-eight.

'There is a Burmese proverb that says a man should marry a woman half his age, plus four years,' he explained with a grin.

So how did he make the leap from gem trader to business owner? When the government declared that 1996 would be 'Visit Myanmar Year', in an effort to boost foreign tourism, Mya Nyunt decided to seize the opportunity. It was an interesting turn for the former NLD organizer, since Aung San Suu Kyi had called on foreign tourists to boycott the country during the tourist promotion campaign. (The government still requires that every day, all hotels must file detailed information on every guest with six agencies: police, immigration, military intelligence, customs, local authorities, and internal revenue.)

Due in part to the opposition leader's exhortations, the 'Visit Myanmar Year' was widely deemed a failure, but Mya Nyunt had already opted for a career change from his lucrative but socially undesirable job as a gem dealer. With the funds he had saved in the gem business and a loan from his mother, Mya Nyunt spent eighteen months building a small hotel in his hometown.

Today he and his wife, who helps run the hotel when she is not caring for their young son, employ eight staff. They have developed a reputation for good service at reasonable prices that occasionally brings foreign tourist groups to the hotel, and business is strong enough that they plan to open a restaurant for lunch and dinner service. He is planning other business ventures as well. It is a far cry from his activist days.

I asked Mya Nyunt to reflect on how today's young Burmese compared with those in his generation. 'They are more afraid than we were,' he said. 'Who can blame them? After all, the government has all the guns and all the power, and they have shown they are not afraid to use it.'

Chapter 4

Cultural Guardians

'I t is actually a good time to be an artist in Burma,' the painter told me. 'The hotels are buying up local art, and putting on exhibits for the tourists. In the past, my painter friends had to live off their wives or daughters. They were working for their next meal. Now they can even afford to have galleries.' He told me about several of his artist friends whose works were being shown in one of Rangoon's few modern high-rise hotels.

The painter spent time in prison in the early 1990s for his involvement in the opposition movement, and said he is still routinely followed. As a result, he plays the games that so many artists and intellectuals in Burma are forced to play these days. To make contact with me, he came to downtown Rangoon more than an hour before our appointment. To throw off any potential followers, he slowly worked his way down the street toward my hotel, stopping in one shop after another, always checking over his shoulder, before he slipped inside the lobby for our rendezvous. He had been watching the downtown street for so long, he could tell me when I walked out of the hotel for lunch nearly an hour before our first meeting. 'I thought it was you,' he said when I introduced myself. 'I saw you cross the street to the noodle shop.'

The artist's story of imprisonment and constant awareness of watchful eyes is not unusual among Burmese artists and intellectuals today. Come to Burma, enjoy the cultural bounty, the government says. Visitors are welcome, even encouraged, to enjoy the 'state approved' culture, which includes gleaming pagodas, centuries' old wall paintings, and ancient stone tablets. They are a magnificent testament to the Burma's rich history and traditions, and many have been spruced up in recent years specifically with tourism in mind. But peel back the layer of government bureaucracy that keeps 'approved' culture in front of most foreign visitors, and where are the people breathing life into the country's artistic and intellectual community? Burma's writers, artists, historians, and other scholars today live in virtual intellectual prisons, their movements monitored by intelligence agents, and their work muzzled by state censors.

Since the violent government crackdown during and after the 1988-89 democracy movement, artists and intellectuals have been among the most closely monitored groups in the country. Many were sent to prison for alleged involvement in the movement, and they remain cowed since being released. Not only is their work screened, but their access to information, ideas and even open conversation – the sustenance of creative and intellectual life – is controlled to a suffocating degree. Foreign travel is tightly restricted, and the state-controlled media are mind numbing.

One way to gauge the current atmosphere is by visiting the teahouses of Rangoon. Burma is famous for her open-air teahouses. They have long been favorite gathering places for the Burmese who, being sociable by nature, while away hours drinking tea and talking with friends. In the past, the teahouses in Rangoon were also popular places for artists, intellectuals and students to meet and debate books, politics or other current issues, much like Parisian cafes in the 1920s.

Today the teahouses are full, generally with men, but the discussions are likely to be about business deals or job prospects, and there are few intellectual conversations to be found. Discussion of politics is strictly forbidden, and plainclothes intelligence agents are on the lookout for potential signs of trouble. I had two such agents sit down at my table uninvited one morning when I pulled out an English-language newspaper in a crowded teahouse in central Rangoon. The men never said a word as they chain-smoked and watched me through dark glasses from across the table. While I had been greeted with welcoming smiles from the other patrons when I first walked into the teahouse, they all averted their eyes once the two silent strangers joined my party.

In the absence of free public discussion and a free press, the intellectual and creative communities are forced to meet clandestinely in friends' homes, exchanging news and ideas in small private gatherings, often under cover of darkness. Most rely on short-wave radios to pick up broadcasts by the BBC World Service in English, as well as Burmese language broadcasts by the BBC, Voice of America, the Democratic Voice of Burma (from Norway), and Radio Free Asia.

Despite the repressive atmosphere, friends in Rangoon told me there was still a small group of people carrying the flickering torch of Burmese cultural and intellectual life. I asked to meet a few of them, in hopes of glimpsing a side of the country that is in danger of being smothered by authoritarian zeal. With few exceptions, most of the artists and intellectuals willing to speak with me were of the older generation. They came of age when Burma was still under British rule, or flush with the excitement of independence, and still remember a time of free speech and expression. Their younger counterparts, many of whom have known nothing but life under the military government that has ruled since 1962, were more reluctant to talk. Yet even the older people chose their words carefully.

One of the men I met in Burma is a writer and scholar who lives behind a high wall on the north side of Rangoon. A friend who knew the scholar agreed to take me to see him. (There were always introductions and escorts in these conversations, I learned.) It was raining the night we went to visit, and after what seemed like an interminable drive in pitch darkness, we turned down a dirt road full of giant potholes that had turned into muddy ponds. There were no streetlights to guide our driver, who futilely tried to navigate around the pools. We bumped and pitched along for about fifteen minutes, until the car stopped in front of a large gate and the driver honked. The gate swung open and we entered a court-yard in front of a rambling bungalow.

The house was filled with stacks of musty manuscripts and papers. We were invited into a living room with pale blue walls that was piled full of books and papers bound with pink plastic twine. A collection of the old man's canes was leaning in one corner, and a large plaster bust of his head was on a table in the opposite corner. (I noted that a number of older, well-educated Burmese had large portraits or busts of themselves on display in their homes.)

'The Professor', a white-haired old man, is a renowned historian. After a distinguished career teaching at the country's top universities, he was allowed to go abroad in the early 1980s to teach at foreign univer-sities. His wife and children stayed behind. The Professor returned to Burma to care for his family following the government crackdown in 1988-89. When I met him, all Burmese universities had been shut down for an extended period due to concern about student demonstrations, and his formal teaching consisted only of meetings with a handful of graduate students.

Nonetheless, he had a small, devoted following among other intel-lectuals and former students, who made regular pilgrimages to his home. Even the middle-aged men among them referred to the Professor rever-entially as 'teacher', showing a respect for scholars that is rooted in Bur-ma's Buddhist heritage.

The Professor's passion is the Early Bagan period, which is widely recognized as the height of Burmese civilization. Bagan is a city in cen-tral Burma that was founded on the banks of the Ayeyarwady River in the ninth century. It reached its zenith two centuries later when King Anawrahta ascended to the throne and formed the first centralized gov-ernment in the land later to become known as Burma. The earliest re-corded written history of Burma began with this period. During an era of tremendous building, the city and surrounding plains were filled with thousands of temples and monuments between the eleventh and thir-teenth centuries. By the end of the thirteenth century, more than 4,400 archeological sites were said to exist within a forty-square kilometer area, making Bagan one of the world's great archeological zones.

Today only half that number exists. Bagan remains a spectacular destination, and is one of the most heavily promoted tourist sites in Burma, but the area's fragile archeological ruins are under threat of further deterioration. A number of forces have struck Bagan over the centuries. Fire destroyed many of the original palaces and monasteries, which were made partly or entirely of wood. The region is also in an earthquake zone, and has suffered a series of shocks through its history. A major quake in 1975 damaged many of the important remaining structures. UNESCO subsequently began a number of restoration projects intended to reinforce the damaged monuments, but it has since discontinued its work. U Chit San said the most recent, and potentially most devastating, threat to Bagan is human.

'The United Nations pulled out of Bagan because the Burmese government is doing nothing to stop its destruction,' the Professor lamented. 'The first time I went to Bagan more than forty years ago, I saw many buildings in various stages of ruin. Since that time, most of those buildings have disappeared.'

In his view, the current problem is due to a combination of Buddhist zeal and a race for tourist dollars. 'The monks only want new buildings on display, they don't want old buildings,' he said. 'You want to offer the best to Buddha, and they think newer is best. They take pride in tearing down the old buildings.' The government, meanwhile, is eager to appease the senior monks and to bring in more tourists to Bagan, he observed.

Ironically, the Professor's interest in his own country's ancient history was sparked by a noted British historian who taught in Burma. The Professor subsequently went to London to study in the 1950s, and the historian asked the young Burmese to carry on his early work on Bagan. It was not until the Professor returned to Burma from London that he actually traveled to Bagan for the first time. He has dedicated his professional life to the subject ever since.

The difficulty in studying the archeological zone, the Professor said, stemmed from the fact that all the original source materials on the Early Bagan period were inscriptions on stone. He and his students subsequently set out to make rubbings of the thousands of script-covered stones that could be carried back to Rangoon on paper for further study.

While we sat in his living room that rainy evening, he left the room for a moment and returned with a series of large, rolled-up scrolls. One by one, he carefully unrolled the scrolls on a low table and smoothed them out in front of him. They were covered with curlicued Burmese script set off against gray-rubbed backgrounds. These were the precious historical texts that he and his coterie of students, past and present, pored over for hours at a time when they gathered at his home. Their interest in the historical detail of Early Bagan was surpassed only by the Professor's anger at the authorities' neglect of the archeological sites.

The old man expressed his concerns about the fate of Bagan in an article he wrote in 1995. Due to government concerns about its publication prior to 1996, dubbed 'Visit Myanmar Year', the document was not released until 1997.

'1996 was supposed to be the year of the visitors,' the Professor said. 'The government did not want this floating around as a public embarrassment. I was only trying to be honest. Now, as far as I am concerned, there's no hope. These people do not know anything about culture. They do not understand renewal and repair.'

Surely there are others inside Burma who are concerned about the destruction of such a great archeological treasure, I suggested. He nodded, gesturing to a few of his current and former students gathered in the room. 'There are people who want to help, but it is not worth trying in the current environment.'

One of the organizations that formerly took an active interest in cultural and preservation issues was the Burma Research Society. Founded in 1910, the Society was the country's leading scholarly organization dedicated to research, documentation and preservation of Burmese customs, history, language and literature, among other topics. The Professor was an active member of the Society, and at a conference to celebrate the group's seventieth anniversary in 1980, he read a paper warning of the destruction of the sites of Bagan.

After the conclusion of the conference, the Professor said, General Ne Win ordered that the venerable Burma Research Society be closed. Didn't anyone question why it was closed, I asked? Was it a political issue, I suggested?

My questions caused the Professor's temper to flare. 'Don't you know it's against the law to discuss such things?' he snapped. Then, recomposing himself, he said simply: 'He is the dictator here. No one had the courage to ask him why he did it.'

The revered elder statesman of Burmese poetry, a man whose writing has been studied by millions of Burmese school children over the decades, is nearly ninety years old now. He has seen much in his lifetime, from the British colonial period (he was one of the few Burmese to study at Oxford University in the 1930s), to World War II and the Japanese occupation, the quest for independence, and all the change that has come since then. We spent several hours together one evening at his Rangoon home, where he spoke about his own childhood, his education, career, and poetry, but avoided questions about current life in Burma. He remained focused, as does his poetry, on a simpler, slower time.

'Although I have been in Rangoon for many years, I have not forgotten my jungle people, my jungle ideas,' he told me. 'My poems for children focus on familiar things: going down to the river, picking ripe fruit, climbing trees. I use simple, everyday language. After all, we Burmese are a simple people at heart. Even today, my language is rural, rustic, colloquial.' He is still contributing poems regularly to a monthly magazine. At the time of my visit, he was writing poetry about birds. The reference books piled on his coffee table included *Birds of Southeast Asia*, and *Trees and Plants of Burma*.

The poet spoke about pride in his national identity, and the desire for independence from Britain that burned within him as a young man. Part of the urge for an independent identity stemmed from his brief stint in the 1930s as the headmaster of an Anglo-Vernacular middle school, where students were taught in both English and Burmese. The curriculum required that students learn poetry in both languages. While there were many poems in English for the children to choose from, there were none in Burmese, he recalled. The young headmaster set out to write verse that would inspire the students to appreciate their own culture and language.

While his writing began with children's poetry, he subsequently published a wide range of works for adults, as well as translating well-known foreign works into Burmese. One of his most formidable accomplishments was a translation of Shakespeare's King Lear, which he worked on for ten years. Today, he remains active not only as a writer, translator and literary historian, but also as an influential member of Rangoon's literary society, which holds regular gatherings at his home.

The poet's popularity among the Burmese people is so great that in the election of 1990, he was overwhelmingly elected to represent a Rangoon district on behalf of the opposition National League for Democracy before the election results were annulled. Many of his fellow opposition candidates were subsequently thrown in jail by the government, but the poet was an old man by that time. Apparently fearing a backlash if they imprisoned such a revered figure, the government put him under surveillance for a number of years. During a more recent crackdown on NLD members, in 1998 he officially resigned from the opposition party, reportedly for health reasons.

Unfortunately, I was not able to discuss any of these events with the poet, because he sharply disavowed any involvement in political issues when I raised the topic during our conversation at his home. 'I am not involved in political things,' he stated, although his eyes told me something different. Instead, I was left to interpret his views by reading between the lines of his remarks, which, like his poetry, often hid political themes in his discussion of other subjects.

If he could share one message with the people of Burma, I asked, what would it be?

'I just want my people to know our own culture, our birds, trees and so on,' the elderly poet said. 'We don't care enough for our surroundings, living or lifeless. But there are things around us which we should know, understand and look after. We need to be careful of our own selves. The people should know this; they must know it. They cannot rely on outside forces.'

Poets are not the only writers in Burma who must exercise caution with their words. 'Almost any piece of writing is subject to the whim of the censors,' a middle-aged journalist told me with exasperation.

The Printers and Publications Registration Act is a source of constant concern for my journalist friend and his colleagues. The act requires all publications, movie scripts, and even song lyrics to be approved by the Burmese government before printing or distribution. The content of all books, newspapers and magazines published in Burma is reviewed by the government's Press Scrutiny Board (PSB), which was established in 1962. Although the PSB started with a relatively narrow purview, its scope and powers have been expanded dramatically. Today the board has a wide-ranging censorship role, and does not hesitate to use it.

A series of guidelines for authors, first put forth by the Ministry of Home and Religious Affairs in 1975 and updated since then, allows the PSB to prohibit the publication of 'anything detrimental to the sovereignty, ideology or objectives of the state; anything which might be harmful to national solidarity and unity; anything which might be harmful to security, the rule of law, peace and public order; any incorrect ideas and opinions which do not accord with the times; any descriptions which, though factually correct, are unsuitable because of the time of their writing; any descriptions which, though factually correct, are unsuitable because of the circumstances of their writing; any obscene (pornographic) writing; any writing which would encourage crimes and unnatural cruelty and violence; any criticism of a non-constructive type of the work of government department; any libel or slander of any individual'.

According to a noted foreign expert on the Burmese press, the list of topics specifically forbidden for publication since 1988 has included: 'democracy, human rights, politics, the events of 1988, senior government officials, the Burmese Socialist Program Party and socialism, the Nobel Peace Prize or anything that might bring Daw Aung San Suu Kyi to mind (such as calling the heroine of a story "Ma Suu"), and any other criticism of the government or of military personnel'. Additional forbidden subjects have been added to the list in the 1990s, including 'any other topic deemed unsuitable to the PSB', and 'anything unambiguous or unclear'.

'The most sensitive subjects are criticism of political and economic decisions made by the junta, criticism of religious topics, and criticism regarding the culture and history of Burma,' my journalist friend said. 'The restriction on these subjects is getting worse and worse at present.'

As a result, writers frequently adopt indirect ways of communicating their messages to readers. 'Sometimes, writing a feature story in Burma is like courting a woman,' a former magazine editor told me. 'Though a man can finish his business by saying three words – "I love you" – he instead sends indirect but repeated messages in his conversation and in his body language because he doesn't know if it will end peacefully, or with a slap in the face, or in a trial for sexual harassment, if it is in America. In the case of the Burmese writer, if he presents his case directly, frankly and effectively, his editor will surely receive more than a slap, and will end up signing a paper printed with these words: "I acknowledge that so and so's story or essay or article was violating the principles laid down by the state. I won't print such a piece of work in my magazine in the future. If I do, I shall be punished by the PSB and I sign here that I understand the punishment." '

Writing stories with 'double meaning' is another common method of trying to avoid censorship, and literary nonfiction has been used by some magazine writers to weave their messages into imaginary settings. The former editor used the following story as an example: 'When one of my friends reported on tourism, a sensitive issue for the government because of its "Visit Myanmar Year" promotion in 1996, he created two characters, a man and a woman, who were tour guides and in love. They happened to be on the same trip, representing different tour groups. The writer mixed love and tour scenery, sketched the character of the tourists, and gave most of the space to the real facts of business, with a moderate dose of criticism on the government's tourism policy here and there in the dialogue. By creating an imaginary love story and characters in the context of a real report to circumvent the censors, he obviously went beyond new journalism and probably beyond even literary nonfiction. Yet no writers in Burma called it fiction, and his editor labeled it a "feature story".'

Another way that writers have skirted the censors is to write about one subject that suggests another subject to the reader. Instead of writing directly about democracy, for example, they might write stories about freedom and individualism. 'I could not speak about freedom,' a journalist told me, 'so I focused on the individual. Democracy is not just politics, it is a way of life.'

When the government censors find a topic or article they disapprove of, the offending article must be removed from the publication prior to distribution. In the past, publications were circulated in the country after particular items had been ripped out or inked over. In 1996, in an apparent attempt to appear less heavy-handed to readers, the PSB instructed publishers that if there was even one word the censors disapproved of, an entire story had to be removed and replaced by a new PSB-approved story that would not make the change apparent to readers. The time required to get a distribution permit for a book increased from three months to more than one year in some cases.

Today the PSB maintains the names of blacklisted writers, said to number about thirty, who have been targeted because they are labeled 'leftists', 'rightists' or are NLD members. The works of these writers are more carefully scrutinized than others, and often banned outright.

For some journalists, the price of speaking out has been more severe. In May 1999, the World Association of Newspapers issued a list of countries ranked according to the number of journalists in prison. Burma ranked fifth on the list with eight known journalists in prison. Writers have been sentenced to as much as twenty years in prison for alleged violations of the Printers and Publications Registration Act.

Meanwhile, the country's official press is expected to defend, protect and extend the legitimacy of military rule. 'The army itself is the news,' my journalist friend explained. 'What the generals say, what they do, what they think and what they do not think are news in official press.'

A retired editor with one of the official government newspapers concurred. 'Your individual opinion is not very important,' he said. 'We are just employees. We serve the state.'

The longtime government editor, who had a stubble of gray beard and a nervous laugh, said he had regularly read foreign newspapers during his two decades working for the state. I asked his opinion of the US papers he had read. 'They are of a high standard, outspoken, and a little biased too,' he said. 'They are against any restrictions, and for complete freedom. But complete freedom is unthinkable to us. We need some sort of guidance. We are a little outdated, a little backward perhaps, but our young people have to be guided and channeled toward the policies of Buddhism and the state.'

Part II
Tradition

Chapter 5

Whispers At The Pagoda

Approaching the shrine in the early morning darkness, I saw hordes of people streaming through the doors. It was just before 4:00 a.m., and Mandalay was still cool in the pre-dawn blackness. I, along with hundreds of Burmese, had come to observe a daily ritual at the Mahamuni Paya, a shrine built to house the celebrated Mahamuni image. Every morning at four o'clock, a team of monks uses cloth and brushes to scrub the gleaming golden face of the four-meter-tall seated Mahamuni, an ancient Buddha image that some believe to be one thousand years old. The Mahamuni, originally cast in bronze, has had so much gold leaf applied to it by worshippers over the centuries that the gold leaf is estimated to be fifteen centimeters thick.

That morning, as every morning, the shrine was filled with hundreds of worshippers, a majority of them women, facing toward the front of the hall where, framed by an elaborately etched, gold-covered wall ringed with colored lights, the team of monks worked on a sort of scaffolding to meticulously clean the Buddha's face. From my position fifty meters away, the shine of its giant gold cheeks and forehead was brilliant.

The worshippers were crammed into the shrine's long, narrow main hall, and appeared oblivious to discomfort as they sat or kneeled on the hard floor in close quarters, bowing low to the Mahamuni with their hands folded and pressed to their foreheads. Near the front of the hall, several male elders of the shrine, dressed in white from head to toe, were seated behind a low table on which they were preparing various offerings for the Mahamuni: rolls, fruit, and flowers. Everyone in the hall appeared transfixed by the face-scrubbing ceremony, and many of them were here on a daily basis. When we left the shrine nearly an hour later, the ceremony was still under way and all of the worshippers remained. Outside, the sky was still black.

The Mahamuni shrine was at the center of a controversy in early 1997 that illustrates not only the powerful role that religion plays in Burma, but also the government's recognition and use of that power. March 1997 was the month in which a series of anti-Muslim riots swept Mandalay, causing serious damage to the city's mosque. According to monks associated with the Mahamuni Paya and others, the story behind the riots began when people tied to the government took precious objects from the shrine complex. The monks and pagoda elders protested. As a diversion, the monks claimed, the government subsequently fomented riots targeting the Muslim community (composed largely of ethnic

Indians) that put Mandalay in an uproar. Several monks and other people independently told me that the government had agents disguised as monks instigate the riots at mosques.

'It was easy for them to pose as monks,' an abbot, or senior monk, told me. 'They just shaved their heads and put on yellow robes. But we Buddhists resent this attempt to distort our image. We are peaceful and non-violent people.'

Indeed, the Burmese generally are a serene, decorous people, reflecting the pervasive Buddhist influence in their country. Buddhism is a religion espousing peace and contentment, and it is woven into the daily lives of millions of Burmese. If one is suffering in this life, Buddhists believe, it is due to *karma*, or 'cause and effect', linked to their deeds in a previous life. Acceptance of one's fate is a central tenet. Buddha taught that in life, even the happiest moments are temporary and unsatisfactory, and that suffering is unavoidable. The root of suffering is said to be in feelings such as desire and greed. The concept of rebirth is an important part of Buddhism, and followers believe that through meditation, they can master their own minds to achieve wisdom, overcome their cravings and achieve happiness. The ultimate goal of every Buddhist is to end the cycle of rebirth and enter into nirvana. Because there is no Buddhist god to pray to for help, one's destiny depends entirely on one's actions.

Buddhism is an essential element of what the people call *bamahsan chin*, or Burmese-ness. It is estimated that more than three-quarters of the Burmese population is Buddhist. Many people, particularly in rural areas, simultaneously pursue traditional beliefs such as *nat*, or 'spirit', worship. More than just a religion, Buddhism is a way of life, and a cultural phenomenon, in Burma.

Sadly, in recent years Buddhism also has been used as a tool of the military government. While glorifying Buddhism as the state religion, the regime has frequently created religious tension to divide the population. An increased military presence in remote regions of the country has resulted in growing religious persecution among ethnic minorities, many of whom are Christian, despite the fact that Burma's 1974 Constitution states that all religions are allowed to be practiced. In heavily Christian areas such as Chin State, for instance, the army has actively harassed and punished those who practice Christianity and rewarded those who convert to Buddhism.

The degree to which Buddhism permeates life in Burma is readily apparent. Buddhist temples, pagodas and monasteries are found in even in the tiniest rural villages. A row of shaven-headed monks in their saffron-colored robes, parading down the roadside in the morning with their alms bowls, is one of the enduring images of this country. Buddhist festivals, timed on the Burmese calendar according to phases of the moon, are widely celebrated by young and old alike. During one of the most important annual festivals, celebrating the end of Buddhist Lent, I saw lights and lanterns hung on pagodas, monasteries and houses around the country, firecrackers were set off, and people flocked to the pagodas in a celebratory mood.

Buddhism plays an important role in Burmese family life as well. Many Buddhist homes contain small altars, where fruit, rice and flowers are offered every day with morning prayers before breakfast. Because Buddhists believe that only a man can become a Buddha, men are accorded some preferential treatment by their wives who, for instance, traditionally wait until their husbands have finished eating before they will have their meal. (This practice is less common among younger couples, and Burmese women pride themselves on their independence and equal rights in society.) Children are also taught to respect their elders, in the Buddhist tradition. The end of Buddhist Lent is also a time of respect for the elderly, and visits are frequently paid to aged relatives and friends.

Most devout Buddhist families send their sons to live at the monastery for a few weeks when they are boys; there, the 'novice' monks don yellow robes and learn the lessons of obedience, discipline and spiritual influence. It is not as prestigious for families to have their daughters become nuns, but when boys are celebrating their entrance into the monastery, it is common for their sisters to have their ears pierced in a special ceremony.

The vast majority of Burmese follow Theravada Buddhism, a school also followed in Thailand, Laos, Cambodia and Sri Lanka. Theravada keeps strictly to the teaching of Lord Buddha as contained in a collection of his writings. Theravada Buddhism differs from Mahayana Buddhism (followed in China, Japan and Vietnam), which is a more broadly based school that borrows from Hinduism and Tantrism. There is evidence that both major forms of Buddhism were practiced in Burma until the eleventh century, when Theravada achieved dominance.

Today only a small percentage of people in Burma, virtually all of Chinese descent, practice Mahayana Buddhism. One difference between the schools that manifests itself on a daily basis is the practice among most Theravada Buddhists of eating meat, while Mahayanas are vegetarian.

Rangoon's Shwedagon Pagoda, the most revered site in Theravada Buddhism, is also the spiritual heart of Burma. Much of the country's religious and political history is closely intertwined with the pagoda complex. It was the first site I visited on my initial visit to Burma, and has been a lure for me ever since. The giant golden pagoda's spire rises dramatically from a hilltop in central Rangoon, and is visible for kilometers around.

To reach Shwedagon on that first visit, a friend and I had to climb one of four long staircases leading to a huge patterned marble platform surrounded by sixty-four open shrines. Many of the covered, open-air shrines were full of ordinary Burmese sitting cross-legged on the floor with their prayer beads, burning incense sticks, or making offerings to Buddha. Looking up, I saw that the base of the steeple's tapered top was surrounded by seven-tiered golden umbrellas that were decorated with tiny bells. I also noticed dark storm clouds gathering in the sky. We wandered on, taking note of the worshippers and vibrant colors around us, the colors made even more brilliant by the gray afternoon light.

When we stopped to watch a couple of teenage girls pour holy water over the heads of small white Buddha images, a slight, gray-haired man in a green-checked *longyi* and short jacket approached us. His skin was dark brown, but his features were more angular than those of many round-faced Burmans. After introducing himself, he told us that he was a retiree in his eighties who visited the pagoda several mornings a week. With little encouragement, he was happy to share some of the pagoda's history with us in British-accented English.

Delighted to have such a well-informed source at our disposal, we asked him a string of questions about Shwedagon, and he clearly enjoyed our interest. After about five minutes, however, a pained look suddenly crossed his face, and his glanced over his shoulder.

'Please, come with me,' he said, pointing us toward one of the covered shrines nearby. As we ascended the steps, I noticed a man in dark glasses standing alone nearby, surveying the crowd. Our new friend led us to the side of the shrine's platform, where we sat on the floor alongside a dozen worshippers praying to a trio of golden Buddhas that were draped in burgundy cloth. The people nearest to us smiled shyly.

Keeping his voice low and occasionally glancing about, our Burmese friend told us that he was born on an island in Rakhine State, the coastal region of west Burma that borders India (that explained his more Indian-looking features). His parents had come to Burma from India during the British colonial period, and he still had fond memories of British rule. He had served in the Burmese military himself for many years, and eventually retired in Rangoon. Now his only contact with the world outside Burma was the occasional letter or phone call from a son, who had left the country some years earlier for Singapore.

After another glance over his shoulder, the old man suddenly lowered his voice so it was barely audible. 'You know of Aung San Suu Kyi?' he asked, whispering the name of the opposition leader. Yes, we replied, leaning in closer. He gave a thin-lipped smile. 'Will you go see her?' he whispered. It was 1996, and Aung San Suu Kyi was giving defiant speeches in front of her home for thousands of followers every weekend. We nodded; yes, we planned to go. He beamed. Our answers seemed to please him, but he said nothing more about politics. The man in dark glasses had disappeared, yet there were too many other people within earshot.

The heavens suddenly opened and a tremendous downpour hit the pagoda complex. It was the most powerful rainstorm I had ever been in. Those who hadn't already done so scurried for cover. The noise on the roof was deafening, and we huddled closer to the worshippers on the floor, trying to avoid the sheets of water that were blowing in under the eaves. Unable to leave the shrine without getting drenched, we spent the next hour in quiet conversation with the old man, who was eager for news from the outside world and interested to learn about our lives. As we talked, several people sitting near us inched closer in hopes of catching a few words, but the pounding rain made it difficult to hear.

When the downpour finally ended and people got up to wander off through the puddles, the old man had one request to make. 'You have heard of this book, *The Satanic Verses?*' he asked us, referring to Salman Rushdie's controversial novel that stirred the wrath of Muslims. We nodded. 'It is not available here in Burma, but I would like very much to receive a copy.' I found it ironic that the sole request of a man standing in this holy Buddhist pagoda was for a book so infamously linked to the Muslim religion.

'When I was a young novice, I wanted to leave the monastery,' the old monk recalled, peering out through large, heavy-framed black glasses. 'My parents insisted that I stay, since they were very poor. They said I could have a better life here.'

That was over fifty years ago. Today he is the abbot of his monastery, as well as a respected writer and scholar. Like many of the country's older, well-educated people – monks and laymen alike – the abbot had his early training in a monastery school. Until early in the twentieth century, monastery schools educated the vast majority of Burmese children. In fact, the Burmese word for school, *kyaung*, is also the word for monastery.

I left my shoes at the entrance, in keeping with Buddhist custom, and sat down with the abbot in a quiet courtyard of the monastery. We were under a latticework trellis covered with thick green vines that shielded us from the blinding morning sun. A chorus of birds chattered overhead. I spotted small lizards and toads moving in the shadows. Several slim cats padded about the courtyard. The abbot sat cross-legged on a rattan mat on a simple, raised wooden platform, his orange robes wrapped loosely around his thin frame. I sat facing him in a deep bamboo chair that was at least sixty centimeters lower than the platform, in keeping with Buddhist custom that women stay on a lower plane than men.

'My parents were right,' the abbot mused. 'If I were not a monk I would be a weaver, like they were, leading a hard working life. I would not be educated or enlightened.'

Most of the young novices and monks in Burma's monasteries today come from humble backgrounds. Life in the monastery may offer them opportunities for a better life, but it is far from comfortable.

'City men generally do not become good monks,' the abbot said. 'They are richer and lead comfortable lives. The rarely come to the monastery, for they know the poor living conditions of a monk.'

The abbot described a Spartan lifestyle in which the monks rise early, study hard, meditate often, eat little (including no solid food after noon) and live in humble surroundings. 'It's not important if the monastery is grand or beautiful,' he said. 'What is important is you get shelter from the heat or cold. Your robe is not meant to be beautiful, it is simply a means to cover yourself. And your food is not meant to be delicious, but is meant to keep you fit and healthy.'

As the elderly monk and I talked, a gray and white spotted cat jumped up on the platform where he was seated. He picked up the cat and gently stroked its back as he spoke, a gesture that seemed to soften his serious demeanor.

The tradition of sending sons to the monastery lives on in Burma primarily among rural Buddhist families. 'In the villages, you still have the old traditions, the customs, and boys still go into the monkhood,' the abbot said. But even in the villages, he acknowledged, fewer boys are becoming monks. Concerted recruiting efforts have been organized in recent years to find young boys to join the monastery.

Burma has an estimated 250,000 monks today, including both those that are ordained for life and those boys whose families send them to the monasteries for brief periods of time to live as novices. In addition to their time as novices, there is another opportunity for Burmese males to take up temporary monastic residence later in life. Some do so as fully ordained monks, or *pongyis*, after the age of twenty, and some Buddhist men occasionally return to the monastery for brief periods throughout their lives. The various opportunities either for a full life in the monkhood, or for shorter stays in the monastery, mean that the vast majority of Buddhist men in Burma have spent some time in their lives wearing the yellow robe.

It is hard to miss the morning parade of monks in most Burmese cities and towns. Not only do they walk the streets and circulate among the crowds each morning in the open-air markets, but they also enter private homes on a daily basis to receive offerings of food. (I was sitting in the Rangoon living room of one Burmese couple when the front door opened without a knock, a young monk entered, greeted the couple's daughter and proceeded to serve himself a helping of rice from the large bowl on the table before letting himself out.) This practice keeps them in very close contact with the Burmese people.

'Just open a monk's begging bowl, and you'll see the economic condition of the people here,' the abbot told me. 'An old monk once said, "If the country becomes poor, the monks and the dogs are the first to starve".'

Occasionally, the situation is reversed: people in need come to some of the larger monasteries seeking food from the monks. The abbot recalled that during the tumultuous, uncertain days of 1988 when no rice was available, up to one hundred people came to his monastery seeking food each day. 'There were even young girls among them,' he said. 'I know they were all very ashamed to beg.'

I asked about the most important role a monk could play in society. 'A monk has to do anything that will benefit the masses of the people,' the abbot said. 'That's the teaching of Buddha.' He paused for a moment, then added: 'When I was young, I didn't understand these words. Only now do I understand them, from my own experience.'

By this time we had spent several hours talking in the courtyard, and had shared a simple lunch of rice and curry with our mutual friends in the abbot's private living quarters. I felt we had established rapport. The abbot has just offered me an opening to broach a more controversial topic. Earlier, I had spotted a photo of the opposition leader Aung San Suu Kyi on the wall of his room, and was eager to ask him about the political situation. But I was also aware that it is a crime for people to discuss politics in Burma.

I composed my next question carefully before speaking: 'Is it possible that the Buddhists' belief in unavoidable suffering has made them too accepting of the repressive regime in this country?'

He paused a long time before answering, glancing for a moment at the Burmese friend who sat with us.

'Two things are important for rulers to bear in mind,' he said. 'Working for the benefit of the masses of people, and the need to rule righteously.' He apparently did not think the military regime was upholding its responsibility on either count. This was as close as the abbot came to openly criticizing the government in our conversation, although he was known to be an active supporter of the opposition cause.

The interplay between religion and politics is undeniable in Burma. During the occasional uprisings that have marked the country's history, Buddhist monks have played a central role. In Mandalay, long considered Burma's religious and cultural center, the monks played a particularly key role in keeping the city from chaos during the pro-democracy demonstrations that swept the country in 1988-89. At the time, the monks supported strike movements by the local people, and served as informal intermediaries with the authorities to keep demonstrators from threatening the army in Mandalay Fort and the police in their barracks. During a period when Rangoon was in chaos, bands of monks acted as a sort of local militia in Mandalay, patrolling the streets and urging merchants to hold their prices steady. Even prisoners who were released were apprehended by the monks and taken to the pagodas for food, clothing and medical care before they were turned over to neighborhood groups for supervision. The monks are widely credited with preventing a repeat of the bloody crackdown and hundreds of deaths that occurred in Rangoon.

In recognition of the monks' power, the government today tries to appease them with donations and temple renovations, the abbot said.

'When temples are very famous, or are in the center of the city, the government voluntarily spends money to renovate them,' he said. 'But they also take the trouble to renovate those temples that might be called "strategic", with big walls around them.' He smiled. 'Some pagodas in Burma really are like fortresses.'

The implication was that the regime is pouring money into these 'strategic' Buddhist sites to keep the monks from using their influence to turn the temples or monasteries into centers of anti-government activity. Meanwhile, he noted, temples and monasteries in rural areas get little attention.

'The abbots have no say in this regard,' the abbot said. 'The authorities do what they please.'

A major turning point in the government's relationship with the Buddhist hierarchy occurred with the formation of the Sangha Council in the 1970s. The council is the Buddhist religion's highest authority to settle disputes (over issues of religion, monasteries, and monks' behavior) in Burma. It is composed of a panel of government-appointed senior monks who act as judges. Lower-level councils of monks also exist at the village, township, district and state levels. The abbot charged that the government had used the Sangha Council's influence to intervene in Buddhist affairs using corrupt means. The problem, he said, was that the judges get cut off from the outside world while serving their terms, and are subject to the influence of the lay people who work for them.

'While they are serving, the judges are forbidden to leave the council area, because people may try to bribe them,' the abbot said. 'But the lay officers who work for them receive lots of money. It's obvious the judges don't receive the money, but the lay people are building houses, and buying new cars. In past disputes between monks that go to the Council, it's never the "right" side that wins, it's the side that pays off the staff. Whoever pays more, wins.'

The government's attempt to influence Buddhist affairs is also evident in a relatively recent law that requires all monks to carry identification cards. For those who violate the principal rules of Buddhism – drinking alcohol or committing adultery, for instance – the Sangha Council may force them to leave the monkhood and return to lay life.

In political cases involving activity perceived to be against the government, the situation is more severe. 'Before, no one dared to arrest monks,' said the abbot. 'Now they will be arrested and punished severely, even without consultation of the Sangha Council.'

A long-standing Buddhist organization – The Young Monks' Association – formerly dealt with religious and social affairs among Burmese monks, and was involved in a variety of political causes too, including independence from Britain. The Young Monks' Association was abolished by the Burmese government in 1988, but still functions in the Thai border areas.

Over the past decade, the government has also harassed monks for their involvement with Aung San Suu Kyi. During 1988-89, when the opposition leader was giving political speeches to thousands of Burmese who gathered outside the gates of her Rangoon home every weekend, monks who attended the speeches were photographed by the authorities, according to the abbot. Once they had identified the monks in attendance, the officials visited their monasteries and gave warnings to their superiors.

'Another time, Daw Suu invited a group of monks to her home for a meal,' the abbot said. 'As a result, their monastery was blacklisted. Now monks dare not go, even if she invites them, because the government will condemn them.'

He suggested there might be a role for Buddhist leaders in negotiating an agreement between the military government and the opposition, but said he was not senior enough to put forth such a proposal.

Has the bloody government crackdown in 1988-89 and subsequent harassment cowed the monks into submission, I asked?

'The attitude of monks toward the government has not changed,' the abbot said. 'If the occasion arises, they are ready to rise up once again.'

Chapter 6

Pulling The Strings

The marionette, a traditional Burmese princess, was dancing life-like across an improvised wooden stage, her beaded costume glittering in the afternoon sun, a coy smile on her shiny white face. My eyes traced the strings from her flowing limbs up to the hands that guided them. The man controlling the spirit of this mini-ature princess was U Nee, a sixty-five-year-old puppet master who twisted and jerked the strings with seemingly effortless confidence. He was putting on this impromptu performance just for me.

I asked to see his hands, which reflected years of hard work and dedication to his craft. The hands were dark brown, with long, bony fingers. But the most noteworthy thing about them was the large callous on top of the ring finger of his left hand. This was the point where a wooden cross bar, passing at an angle under his index and middle fingers and over his ring finger, rubbed as it controlled the strings that held the weight of his puppet's body. There was no cal-lous on the right hand, which controlled several more loose strings (minus the crossbar) that attached to the puppet's limbs.

'When you start with the marionettes, it bleeds a lot,' he said of the callused finger. 'Then, over time, it stops bleeding' as the finger toughens up.

U Nee's hands have had decades to toughen. Gray-haired and bespec-tacled with a slight build and ramrod straight posture, he began as a puppeteer at age eighteen, when he apprenticed with one of the best-known troupes in Upper Burma. At the time, he was earning six kyats a night to perform with a troupe that toured the country, performing 180 nights a year. Marionette shows were considered much more than enter-tainment then. They were also an information source, since each show was preceded by a performance of jesters who passed along news from one town to the next.

Marionette theater – yok-thei pwe – is still widely considered the highest form of performance art in Burma, a country known for its love of theater. Noted for its action, refined dialogue and elaborately dressed characters, marionette theater has entertained crowds in Burma for more than two hundred years. The art reached its peak in the nineteenth century, when the Burmese kings regularly enjoyed performances in their palace at Mandalay, a city still regarded as the center of traditional Burmese culture. Lesser stages were constructed for simultaneous performances outside the palace for local people and staff. Traditionally, marionette performances lasted for several nights in a row, generally starting after dark and continuing until sunrise each day.

But time took its toll on marionette theater after the last Burmese king was deposed by the British in the late 1800s. The introduction of cinema in the 1930s lured away some of the audience, and the Japanese occupation during World War II cut attendance further. With the growing popularity of television in recent years, the art form has practically died out across the country. Most people in Burma under the age of thirty-five have never seen a live performance. U Nee and his troupe are part of a small band of artists trying to revive the traditional art form.

Buoyed by the small but growing number of foreign tourists seeking local culture and entertainment in Burma, a few troupes today put on short evening shows that include highlights from the traditional all-night performances. U Nee is part of a troupe put together in 1991 by U Tin Gyi and Daw Mi Mi Tun, a husband-and-wife team. ('U' and 'Daw' are honorifics commonly used for men and married women, respectively.) The couple started the troupe after Daw Mi Mi Tun decided to supplement her teacher's income by opening a craft shop that sold puppets to tourists.

'One day a foreign couple came into the shop and asked me to demonstrate the puppets,' Daw Mi Mi Tun recalled. 'I was embarrassed that I didn't know how. The lady said she would come back in a year and buy a puppet if I could show her how to manipulate it.'

Prodded by the encounter, Daw Mi Mi Tun sought out a puppet master and began studying marionette theater. As she became more involved in the art form, she realized it might appeal to a broader audience. She and her husband decided to pool their resources and assemble a small puppet troupe.

She recalled the difficulty they encountered in the troupe's early years. Their aim was to target foreign visitors to Burma, but the state ministry of tourism was initially nervous about the prospect of foreigners gathered in their theater, and barred official guides from taking their guests to the show. Daw Mi Mi Tun resorted to passing out leaflets at cultural sites frequented by tourists, and invited people to come for free if they would refer others to the show. After all, she recalled, she had already hired three master puppeteers and was desperate for an audience.

Despite the rocky start, the troupe developed a good reputation, its audience grew, and the state tourism officials eventually relaxed. Today the troupe is thriving, with about twenty performers, not including musicians. U Nee is the only member to have 'master' status, and is clearly revered by the younger performers. Even U Tin Gyi and Daw Mi Mi Tun spoke of his skills in awed tones.

'His movements are so lifelike, as if it's really a human being on stage,' U Tin Gyi said of U Nee's puppetry. 'He can manipulate any one of the puppets in our show.' The standard troupe for a master puppeteer includes twenty-eight characters, ranging from a prince and princess, to a hermit, an alchemist, a horse and a serpent.

Now that their troupe is established, U Tin Gyi and Daw Mi Mi Tun have decided to attempt full-length marionette performances for crowds of local people, much like the old days under the kings.

It is not a simple undertaking. The cost and logistics involved in putting on a full-scale marionette show are considerable, with a total of forty people involved both on-stage and off. Physical demands on the performers are considerable, too. U Tin Gyi, a burly, middle-aged man with a ready smile, said he was physically drained after an all-night performance.

'I am drenched by the end of it,' he said. 'My muscles are sore and I am very, very hot.' His wife spoke of developing her upper body strength in order to maintain control over puppets, her arms outstretched for hours on end.

When I met them for the first time, the troupe was preparing for three successive, all-night shows at a pagoda festival in Upper Burma. The festival was being sponsored by the pagoda committee to celebrate the end of Buddhist Lent, a festival known throughout the country as Thadingyut. Three months of Lenten restrictions – on weddings, travel for monks, traditional ear-boring ceremonies for young girls, and other festivities – had been lifted, and this heavily Buddhist country was in a celebratory mood. Lights adorned homes, verandahs and pagodas, and firecrackers were set off around town.

Having been introduced to U Tin Gyi and his wife through a family friend, I was invited to join them on the second night of the pagoda festival. I climbed into the front seat of U Tin Gyi's pickup truck, and we rumbled off into the star-filled autumn night. The crowds got thicker as we neared the pagoda on the outskirts of town. It was pitch dark, but the headlights of our pickup illuminated clusters of young monks and teenagers streaming toward the pagoda. We passed crude wooden bullock carts carrying families who had traveled hours from the countryside to attend the festival. The traffic eventually backed up until we were at a complete standstill, and a group of performers – musicians and puppeteers – climbed out from the rear of our truck and sprinted through the crowds with their instruments and gear. They were running late, but then, the Burmese are known for a generally relaxed attitude toward time.

U Tin Gyi urged me to get out, too, while he hunted for a parking space. I climbed out of the truck and was immediately swallowed by a friendly crowd moving forward en masse. I was carried along with them until I found myself standing on the edge of a large field that was illuminated by spotlights.

Ringed by a line of wooden carts, lounging water buffalo and bicycle trishaws parked along the back fence, a patient, chattering crowd of several hundred people was sitting on the ground around a large bamboo stage, waiting for the show to begin.

It was a fairly young crowd, including lots of families with children. There were a large number of country people, looking both excited and bewildered by all the activity. Many of the women and children had cheeks and noses dabbed with thanaka, a pasty natural cosmetic (said to soften and protect the skin) that is made from tree bark. A few clusters of young men in leather jackets stood near the back, smoking. In the distance, I saw a good number of food stalls, a night market and other attractions set up next to the pagoda grounds.

I picked out a tiny patch of ground near the back of the crowd, next to a mother and her young son, and sat down cross-legged in their midst, trying to look inconspicuous. Nevertheless, as the only non-Asian in the crowd, a blonde and a woman alone, I was definitely the focus of a lot of attention. The little boy sitting with his mother in front of me couldn't stop staring. I smiled. I was getting used to it.

Then the orchestra struck up. It was a traditional Burmese group, dominated by percussion instruments, that sounded extremely free-form and non-melodic to Western ears. Suddenly, everyone turned their attention to the stage, with its billowing gold curtain and loudspeakers on either side. A hush descended on the crowd as the curtain rose and a pair of dancing marionettes bounded into view. They moved and twirled with humanlike agility. The first act featured a Burmese prince and princess, dressed in elaborate costumes. Next came a horse and a serpent, engaged in frolicsome play. The audience was delighted.

After several scenes, the curtain lifted higher for a minute to reveal the people in control of the puppets. The young men were dressed in traditional outfits: white headbands and neat white, collarless shirts above their tightly wrapped cotton *longyis*. Their hands and fingers were moving in rapid succession.

All of the puppeteers that evening were men. Indeed, a limited number of women have performed in the marionette theater only in very recent years, due to the art's roots in the royal palace and the Buddhist prohibition against women being on a higher level than the king.

The stories told in Burmese marionette theater are typically traditional morality plays. But that night's show also included a few newer scenes created by U Tin Gyi. 'I'm afraid people might get bored if we only perform the old tales,' he had told me earlier. 'I want to appeal to the young people, too.'

Half an hour after the show began, one of U Tin Gyi's assistants found me in the crowd and urged me to come up on the side of the stage. I carefully made my way up a bamboo plank that had been propped alongside the side of the structure, and walked into the backstage chaos of a show in progress. The young man led me to the side of the stage and gestured for me to sit down on a narrow space behind a piece of hanging cloth, just a few inches out of sight of the crowd.

From my vantage point, I could look directly across the stage with a clear view not only of the marionettes, but also of the puppeteers who were working magic with the strings. Arms outstretched and bouncing, they looked as if they were dancing, minus partners, except for the constant motion of wrists and fingers twisting. All of this was hidden from the audience, except for the occasions when the curtain was briefly lifted. The young man working the ropes for the curtain and sets stood directly behind me on a bamboo support structure, nonchalantly smoking a hand-rolled cheroot.

When I got up to stretch, I ran into U Nee backstage. When he was not issuing orders to the young stagehands who were moving props too slowly for his liking, he was warming up his fingers and limbs with Princess Mindon Mye, the marionette character he was most fond of playing. He told me that he still sings all the female parts himself, a practice carried on for generations in this previously all-male craft.

A high point of the evening, not only for the audience, but also the troupe, came when U Nee took the stage. He was playing the alchemist this evening. The marionette was dressed in a deep red costume and had his arms raised to balance a cane behind his head. The figure leapt on stage, and immediately captivated the crowd with the grace and agility of his movements. The troupe's young puppeteers were huddled around me on the side of the stage, absorbing every move.

The highlight of the performance came when U Nee flipped the alchemist's cane down from behind his head and twirled it around as he circled the stage. From my vantage point at the edge of the stage, I saw U Nee's hands spinning over and over as he tossed, caught and released strings that kept the marionette turning without pause. The young puppeteers around me were gasping in awe.

In an earlier conversation, I had asked U Nee what made a good puppeteer. 'A willing mind, and concentration,' he had replied. His face was so concentrated it looked like it could crack during the alchemist's finale.

While everyone was focused on the stage during this performance, the audience's attention did wander later in the evening. But marionette theater has long been a people's art, with little pretense about it. Not every member of the audience is expected to pay attention – or even stay awake – during the entire all-night show. They did follow the action closely enough to anticipate the dramatic high points, however, and the vast majority of people would stay until sunrise.

I was not one of them.

Shortly after midnight, I asked one of U Tin Gyi's young assistants if he could help me find a bicycle trishaw. He disappeared into the crowd, and returned ten minutes later.

Leading me by the hand, he guided me carefully through the mass of people sitting on the ground. When we reached the back of the crowd, he pulled me under the crossbeam of a wooden ox cart. My head was within fifteen centimeters of the animal's hind legs, but I managed to slide past without provoking a reaction. We wandered out past the food vendors and night market stalls to a young man waiting with his bicycle trishaw on the fringes of the crowd.

Once I climbed into the forward seat beside the trishaw driver – my friend took the seat facing rear, with his back against mine – we pushed off into the black night.

As we left the festival crowd behind us, I heard the orchestra strike up another discordant tune in the distance.

Chapter 7

Remembering The British

The road to Candacraig had been a dusty one. By the time the dented green pickup truck rattled to a stop in front of the sprawling old hotel, disgorging two of us and our backpacks from the truck bed, we were covered in grime and full of weary anticipation. After all, the prospect of a stay at Candacraig – built at the turn of the century in the style of an English country mansion by the Bombay Burmah Trading Company – was the main reason we had convinced a groggy Burmese driver to leave Mandalay before sunrise to carry us up several hours' worth of hairpin turns bound for the former 'hill station' of Maymyo.

The pleasant little town, a cool mountain retreat that was the summer capital of colonial Burma, was sought out in the past by British administrators, military men (its namesake was a Colonel May), and other Europeans wilting from heat and humidity on the plains below. The town was renamed Pyin U Lwin several years ago by a Burmese government zealously determined to reinstate pre-colonial place names (foreign tongues be damned). Candacraig, too, had been given a Burmese label, and the stately old lodge was now officially known as the Thiri Myaing Hotel, according to the sign in front, though we never heard a single person, staff or otherwise, refer to it as such.

I had wanted to visit Candacraig as soon as I read about it. The rambling old structure had a colorful past, steeped in the tradition of British colonialism. In the late nineteenth and early twentieth centuries, the Bombay Burmah Trading Company dominated the harvest and transport of teak in Upper Burma, which has one of the largest teak reserves in the world. The Bombine, as the company was known, was one of the pioneering enterprises scattered throughout the British Empire that prospered by sending fresh-faced young men out to far-flung corners of the globe to oversee the harvest and transport of one crop or another in Her Majesty's name. The Bombine's foreign staff was recruited from Britain's top universities, notably Oxford. The firm's underlying philosophy on staffing was that no one was better suited to handle long, difficult, and often solitary stretches in the jungle than the completely educated man. The Bombine had a remarkably low turnover rate.

Teak logging was a difficult, sweaty operation that relied heavily upon elephants which, coaxed and prodded by their Burmese masters, hauled logs out of the tropical forests that were then transported down to the flatlands and were shipped off to build the mansions of colonial India, or carved to decorate the drawing rooms of wealthy Europeans. Unlike the

Burmese, The Bombine's British staff did enjoy an occasional reprieve
from the jungle.

To provide for the rest and relaxation of its expatriate bachelors, The
Bombine built a rambling, two-story lodge on the outskirts of Maymyo,
a cool hilltop town at more than a thousand meters elevation. Constructed just after the turn of the century, Candacraig was built with high
ceilings, fireplaces in the lobby and every bedroom, a sweeping stair-
case up to the second floor landing, woodwork carved in intricate detail,
and private balconies overlooking the spacious lawn. The idea was to
assure that, whatever else may befall them in this foreign land, young
Englishmen in the Bombine's employ could emerge from the jungle to
rediscover the familiar at Candacraig, where a good fire and a plate of
roast beef awaited them every evening they were nestled in its embrace.

By the time my traveling companion and I pulled up in front of
Candacraig, much of the grand old lady's glory had faded. Outside, the
tennis court was net-less and sprouting weeds. Inside, the old rotary dial
phone worked sporadically at best, and the frequent power outages meant
the night watchman had to lead us around with a flashlight. Three decades under socialism had taken a toll. Never mind. Thanks to a handful
of longtime staff who spoke in hushed, almost reverential tones about
their long years of service, Candacraig had retained a comfortable fa-
miliarity, like a patched old hand-me-down that feels as if it had never
belonged to anyone else.

Our host at Candacraig, in spirit if not in title, was James, the maud-
lin old head waiter in an ill-fitting polyester suit. James, who had taken a
Christian name while attending a missionary school, clung to a rosy-
eyed view of the colonial era as dearly as he clung to his outdated clothing. 'They were good to us,' he said of the British, when I engaged him
in conversation on the veranda one afternoon (he always seemed close
at hand). 'They treated us fairly. I was a boy and didn't appreciated it at
the time, but I remember those days very fondly now.'

James seemed impatient at times with the younger waiters, who were
not nearly as attentive as he was to guests in the hotel dining room. His
pride in his work was very evident, and made every effort to please us.
He apologized profusely one night when we found an insect in a drinking glass. The hotel, he told us, was his 'family'.

Recounting Candacraig's transformation from British hostelry to state-
owned hotel as he fawned over us at dinner one night, James said that,
for some years after Burma gained independence in 1948, the property
had been abandoned. Untamed jungle was allowed to swallow the lawn.
'It grew until it reached the second-floor balconies,' James recalled.

Finally, the Burmese government realized that nostalgia sells, especially with foreign tourists. Candacraig was reopened as a state-owned

hotel with a spiffy coat of barn-red paint, complete with many touches borrowed not so subtly from the former colonialists. By the time we arrived, the rooms were sold out most nights to foreigners seeking a taste of the British colonial experience.

During our stay at Candacraig, we were offered afternoon tea on the breezy verandah, or on the lawn, if we preferred. In the formal dining room, James explained, the lunch and dinner menus featured two items, and two items only: roast beef and roast chicken, with gravy, potatoes and steamed vegetables on the side. It was wonderfully nostalgic, but not terribly tasty and got tiresome after a day or so. I thought I would surely stump the waitstaff by ordering a gin and tonic one evening, but they cheerily complied.

Compared to their extended presence in neighboring India, the British did not stay particularly long in Burma. Only sixty-two years passed from the time they deposed the last Burmese king, Thibaw, and annexed Upper Burma in 1886 (completing a takeover of the entire country) to the time they granted Burma independence in 1948. The British had annexed portions of the Burma coast as early as the 1820s and had a long-standing trade in teak and other commodities, but they were less rooted in Burma in those early years. For much of the colonial era, in fact, Burma was governed under British India, and it was not detached from India to form a separate colony until 1937.

Today most tangible evidence of British rule is concentrated in Rangoon, which had more Indian than Burmese inhabitants when the British were in charge. The capital city has its share of moldy colonial-era buildings, many of which now house government offices, and the famed Strand Hotel (whose builders also constructed the Raffles in Singapore and Eastern and Oriental in Penang) has been renovated in recent years. But elsewhere in the country, Maymyo is one of the few places with any real colonial flavor left.

Candacraig may have offered the most nostalgic experience in Maymyo, but the entire neighborhood around it seemed frozen in time. A series of large, Tudor-style 'cottages' with ample lawns, once the official residences of British administrators, lined the winding, tree-shaded lanes on the outskirts of town; the Christian churches nearby were in need of fresh paint but still welcomed worshippers each Sunday morning; the Maymyo Golf Club's grounds were well-maintained, used now by senior Burmese army officers instead of Europeans; the Botanical Garden's rose garden and manicured lawns, built and landscaped during World War I by prisoners of war under British supervision, looked as

English as ever; smiling drivers tried to lure us into their colorful horse-drawn carriages, which were introduced by the British and still ply the roads around Maymyo; and last but not least, the clock tower in the center of town, a gift from Queen Victoria, still chimed regularly.

Although the British have long since departed, they left an impression on the people of Maymyo as well. At one point during our visit, an elderly Burmese woman with gold-capped teeth and shining eyes approached us in a market on the edge of town. In fluent English, she introduced herself and invited us to join her for a cup of tea. She led us to a low table and some tiny stools under the shade of a reaching tree outside the bustling market. Auntie Maureen, as she asked us to call her, was an upbeat, energetic woman of eighty-five. She remembered the British era well. 'It was an exciting time in Maymyo,' she said. 'So many people coming and going.' Her deceased husband had been half-Indian and half-Irish, reflecting the diverse cultural influences in the town. He had come to Maymyo with the military, as so many young men did, and decided to stay. As a lifelong resident of Maymyo, Auntie Maureen could not imagine living anywhere else. Her children were scattered though; one daughter had emigrated to Australia, a son was a soldier in Rangoon, and two other daughters lived with her in Maymyo.

A devout Christian – she attended the Anglican church in town – the old woman repeatedly sprinkled her conversation with phrases like 'thanks to God', and insisted on giving me a plastic crucifix as a gift. She had had little formal education and was extremely poor, yet like James, she chose to overlook life's difficulties and cling instead to happy memories. Her kindness and generosity were obvious.

On a later visit to Maymyo, I went back to see Auntie Maureen and she insisted on making a meal for me. I arrived at her simple home for breakfast at nine o'clock in the morning to find the table covered with every 'English' dish she had learned to make as a girl: roast beef, steamed fish, boiled potatoes, boiled cabbage, stewed beets, and soup, all to be washed down with strong coffee. It was an enormous meal that had probably cost the family's food budget for a month, but she insisted that it was all for me. Auntie Maureen's daughters, whom I met on that occasion, were reserved, rather sober women in comparison to their spry, upbeat mother.

But not everyone in Maymyo was living in the past. The scene near the clock tower revealed the new faces of Maymyo. The central market, just around the corner from the tower, was a vast thicket of stalls selling everything from local produce and fish, to flimsy tennis shoes smuggled in from China, and 'authentic antique' Burmese marionettes that looked like new. The crowd was more multi-ethnic than in other Burmese markets we had visited, and the market had a frontier feel to it.

Little old ladies smoking hand-rolled cheroots and nine-year-old monks in orange robes rubbed shoulders with brash young Chinese men who had just hopped off heavily loaded pickup trucks inbound from the nearby border, and Muslim traders looking to haggle. There were also rosy-cheeked young women selling brilliant flowers, for which this town is famous.

At one point, we sought refuge in a nearby teahouse. Sipping chicory coffee and snacking on *samosas* (the triangular pastries stuffed with a spicy potato mixture introduced to Burma by the Indians), we looked around the room of rough-hewn wood tables and chairs which was filled with elderly Chinese men with wispy beards, a cluster of young Indians engaged in heated discussion, and novice monks circulating from table to table, holding out their shiny black bowls in a silent request for donations. My friend and I were the only women in the room. Adding to the curious mix, the radio played a syrupy rendition of 'I Can't Help Falling in Love With You,' and the walls were plastered with posters of James Bond promoting '555 Brand' cigarettes.

We plunged back into the market crowds for a time, and then made a visit to the local Chinese temple, but after a full day in town, we eagerly returned to the quiet and comfort of Candacraig by late afternoon.

Stepping back in time once more, we lit candles to brighten our room since the power was out again, paid ten kyat per bucket for hot water (available for only two hours in the evening, the water was heated over a cooking fire in the kitchen and delivered to our room in tin buckets by one of the staff), and each took a turn in the bathtub. I located an old tin cup on one of the ledges and began mixing my own blend of bathwater, one part boiling water to one icy blast from the shower head, which I then gently stirred and poured over myself in the candlelight. As I stepped out of the tub, James' voice came floating down the hall, letting the guests know it was time for dinner. Roast beef or roast chicken, of course.

Part III
Today's Struggles

Chapter 8

Serving The New Colonialists

Stepping out of the blinding midday sun, I paused for a moment on the threshold, giving my eyes time to adjust to the dimness inside. Slowly, details of the bustling dining room emerged, and I took a table near the front of what was reputed to be one of the best Shan restaurants in town. Surveying the crowd, I noted that most of the other patrons appeared to be Burmese families chattering over the hearty lunches they shared around big, circular tables. I eagerly ordered a bowl of *Shan khauk-swe*, the popular Shan-style soup made with thin wheat noodles and chili-marinated chicken in a broth.

Then I noticed a table at the back of the room, set somewhat apart from the rest. Around it sat three young men in military uniforms, matching briefcases set on the floor beside them. They could have passed for fifteen or sixteen, but were probably a few years older than that, since their uniforms indicated they were students at the military academy on the edge of town. Looking rather uncomfortable in the stiff collars, the trio kept their heads were bent low, eyes intently focused on the bowls of noodles they were slurping down, as if each of them was in his own little world. I never saw them utter a word to each other, but the young man facing in my direction did steal a glance at me at one point. He looked back down into his noodles as soon as I made eye contact, and did not look up again.

No one else in the restaurant seemed to pay the least bit of attention to them, and it was clear that these young officers-to-be had set themselves apart from the rest of the crowd. They certainly seemed to feel awkward about being there among the masses.

The officer class has set itself apart in numerous ways in Burma. For bright young men today, military careers offer the surest path to a good education, opportunities for advancement, and privilege. Unfortunately, it comes at great expense to the rest of the population.

Members of the military elite are the country's new colonialists. They control not only the guns and government, but also much of the nation's commercial activity and abundant natural resources. Army officers and their families get the best medical care at special military hospitals, ride first class on trains, and play golf on the weekends. Sons and daughters of the officers go to the best schools, get into top universities, and have the opportunity to travel abroad.

Just down the road from the Shan restaurant where I encountered the young military officers, a huge red billboard with white lettering loomed over a key intersection. Similar billboards are scattered throughout the country. 'The Tatmadaw shall never betray the national cause,' it proclaimed in both Burmese and English. The message was hard to miss: Should anyone doubt it, the *Tatmadaw*, or armed forces, are united and firmly in control of Burma.

The Burmese military buildup over the past decade – from 186,000 troops in 1988 to more than 400,000 in 1998, with a goal of 500,000 troops by the year 2000 – gives Burma one of the largest armies in Southeast Asia (this for a country of only forty-six million people). Neighboring China has been a major supplier of tanks, missiles, guns, trucks, aircraft and patrol boats to the Burmese military, while Singapore has assisted in upgrading computer and technical equipment at Burma's regional military command centers.

Yet the military's role goes well beyond defense of the nation. The armed forces have governed Burma since a coup in 1962. They see themselves as the glue that holds the country together. Since independence in 1948, Burma's armed forces have focused most of their energies on fighting internal rebellions and dissonance.

But the forces have also been used to put down peaceful movements, including the pro-democracy demonstrations of 1988-9. The significant troop buildup since 1988, driven in part by the unease those demonstrations provoked among senior officers, seems intended to assure the military's grip on power. By some analysts' estimates (official figures are hard to come by) one-third to one-half of Burma's national budget is now consumed by the military.

Most of the Burmese people express a general disdain for the armed forces. Their views stem not only from the past bloody crackdowns on peaceful demonstrators, but also the widespread curtailment of civil liberties, the concentration of the nation's wealth in a few top officers' hands, and the strangling of the national economy under military rule. Corruption and kickbacks are rife among the top officers.

Yet further probing revealed that the public disdain for the military is, in fact, targeted primarily at the officers who enjoy most of the privileges. Many people expressed pity for the enlisted men who are the foot soldiers in Burma's long-running war against itself. Their morale is known to be low, resentment runs high, and desertions have increased in recent years.

I found myself wondering about a typical soldier's perspective. Shortly thereafter, I met Bo Shwe.

We had been walking since dawn. We were hiking up a steep, rutted dirt path in the sweltering sun, branches thwacking across my face. My feet ached, my legs were sore and I was perspiring profusely, despite the layers of clothing I had shed since we set out in the early morning dew. Up ahead, Bo Shwe had not slowed his pace one bit. His spindly legs were covered in army-green fatigues, and he was wearing a thick wool sweater that he would not take off until we reach the top of the range in the early afternoon. Although he was sixty-one years old, he looked and moved like a man twenty years younger, with an impish grin that brought crinkles to the corner of his eyes.

Bo Shwe spent his entire career in the Burmese Army. Although he never left the enlisted ranks, his years of service and seniority earned him the title 'Bo', or leader, a title commonly used for military officers or commanders. Now six months into retirement, I met him through friends who knew that I was curious to speak with a soldier. They assured me that no one currently in the military would risk such an encounter with a foreigner, but suggested the recently retired Bo Shwe instead.

A daylong hike into the hills near his hometown in Upper Burma was the perfect occasion to establish rapport, assuming I could keep up with his brisk pace. Bo Shwe knew these hills very well, and proved to be an excellent hiking companion. As the day wore on, I realized he was one of the most outgoing, cheerful people I had met in Burma. It was unexpected and rather disconcerting, given everything I had heard about the military. I could not help but like him.

I was also impressed. Not only did he seem to know every villager we encountered on the hike, but his years crisscrossing Burma with the military had also given him formidable language skills. Bo Shwe, who was of Nepalese origin, spoke Burmese, Nepalese, Hindi, the Chin and Kachin dialects, and some English. Reflecting a childhood spent in India, he frequently referred to sums of money in *rupees* rather than the Burmese *kyat*.

He recounted pieces of his life bit by bit throughout the day, as we made our way past clear, bubbling streams, water buffalo lounging in the shade, and villagers carrying fruit, vegetables and tea to market along the winding, worn dirt footpaths in the hills. In a number of ways, I realized, he may not have been a typical soldier, but he nonetheless provided more insights into the life of an enlisted man than I had heard elsewhere.

Bo Shwe was born in 1935 in Chin State, a remote, hilly region in western Burma that borders Bangladesh and India. His parents were Nepalese who came to Burma as most of the country's Nepalese did, with the British Army. The British relied on Nepalese Gurkhas, known to be fierce mountain fighters, throughout their far-flung colonial Empire.

Even today, fifty years after Burma's independence, Nepalese soldiers are still highly sought after in the army ranks. The Nepalese community in Burma lives primarily in the hill regions ringing the country, with concentrations found in the former British 'hill stations', cool highland towns that have long been favored by army officers and colonial administrators.

'Gurkhas prefer cool,' Bo Shwe said with a grin. I noticed that he was perspiring, but he declined to remove the military-issue wool sweater. I could only guess that it was going to get warmer in the hills.

Burma was under British rule when Bo Shwe was born. His father was a soldier in the British Army who spent months at a time away from the family. The Japanese invaded Burma in December 1941, when the boy was six years old, and the British were driven out. Bo Shwe fled to India with his mother and three siblings. They stayed for six years, moving from one refugee camp to the next every six months.

The discontinuity of life as a refugee apparently did not faze the boy. Now, half a century later, he still retained a clear fondness for the daily rituals in the British-run camps.

'I loved the bugle every morning,' he recalled in his broken, heavily accented English.

The war years had a lasting impact on the Burmese of Bo Shwe's generation. It left them with sharp survival instincts, anti-Japanese feeling and, at least in his case, a clear pro-British sentiment.

The family did not return to Burma until 1947, when the country held its first national elections as a prelude to independence the following year. Having settled again in Chin State, they remained poor. Bo Shwe made it through a few more years of school. He was eager to work, but there were few job prospects in the area. The young man had seen many of his Chin friends join the army. The ethnic Chin people had had a long military tradition (including service in the Burmese army when it was under British rule) and today remain prominent among the rank-and-file of the *Tatmadaw*. In 1954, Bo Shwe turned eighteen and joined the Burmese Army.

'I had no other options,' he said matter-of-factly and without apology. Throughout our conversation, he projected an obvious pride in the military tradition within his family.

The country was still flush with the excitement of independence when Bo Shwe joined the ranks, and the military was full of idealistic young recruits ready to fight for their nation. Bo Shwe's first assignment as an infantryman was in the Shan State, where Communist rebels were fighting to overthrow the government. (The region is perhaps best known to Westerners as one end of the old Burma Road, a 480 kilometer supply route cut from the jungle-covered mountainsides in 1938, and along which supplies were shipped from northern Shan State into China's Yunnan Province to supply Chinese troops in their fight against the Japanese.)

'I was so afraid the first time I went into battle,' Bo Shwe recalled. He learned to deal with the fear, he said, but it never left him entirely.

As so many soldiers did, Bo Shwe moved around the country over the years. During a posting in Maymyo, Bo Shwe met his wife, who is also of Nepalese descent. She was working as a teacher at the time. They were married but, like his parents before them, the couple were frequently apart for stretches of six months to a year. They eventually had three children, who are now grown, but Bo Shwe spoke little of his family. Most of his life had been spent apart from them, fighting in the remote hills that ring this country like a horseshoe.

'I have battled the Communists, the Karen, the Shan and others, often deep in the jungle,' he said. 'I go where the army tells me to go.'

As a nation with numerous minority groups and more than one hundred languages, in addition to the ethnic Burman majority, Burma has been plagued with discord since it gained independence. Unlike the British colonizers, who generally allowed minority ethnic tribes in the hill regions to pursue self-governance while they concentrated their control in the central portion of the country, the Burmese army has taken a much more aggressive stance toward minority groups.

A key influence in modern Burma's history has been the military leadership's use of threats to national unity, real or perceived, to justify its powerful role in society. It was an apparent inclination in 1962 by then-national leader U Nu to consider independence for some minority groups that spurred the military coup led by General Ne Win, then head of the armed forces. The resulting military government started the country down the 'Burmese Path to Socialism', a program that has been widely attributed for turning what was once the world's third-largest rice exporter into an inward-looking country forced to seek *less developed nation* status from the World Bank. General Ne Win, although now officially retired in his old age, still wields enormous influence behind the scenes.

Since 1962, the army has increasingly shifted its focus from being protector of the nation to exploiter of her people and resources. Yet the power and accompanying riches are concentrated in very few hands. The backbone of the Burmese military remains the hundreds of thousands of common soldiers, most of them country boys like Bo Shwe was. Driven by poverty and dire circumstances, most have joined the ranks as a means of escape from rural life. It has been their very youth, naiveté and, often, desperation, that has made them such pliant soldiers. From the time they have joined the military, they are kept isolated from the general population, an attempt to keep them from sympathizing with the local people.

Today, Bo Shwe said, enlisted men receive a regular salary, meals, a uniform, and housing. In more remote regions where a large number of troops are deployed, however, rations may only be received sporadically, a situation that has led to an increase in the looting of villagers' food and belongings, as well as demands for money. Army privates earn 600 kyat a month, with salaries increasing to 1,400 kyat for a senior enlisted man. Bo Shwe, who retired at the most senior level an enlisted man can attain, said he receives 1,400 kyat per month in military pension. But even officers' salaries only range from 1,400 kyat to 1,800 kyat a month.

With salaries like that, how is it that the military officers control so much of the country's wealth, I asked?

'Ah,' said Bo Shwe with a smile. 'It's not the salaries, it is the side business.'

The sun had climbed high in the sky. We had reached the top of the range after four hours of hiking, and took a break for lunch with a group of Buddhist nuns at a monastery on the edge of a little village. The nuns set out short, plump bananas, rice with vegetables, and strong black tea on a rough wood plank table, declining to join us but happy for the company. Bo Shwe brought them news from town, and inquired about happenings in the village.

The half dozen nuns, all with shaven heads and bright pink robes, were curious to know about the blue-eyed American woman. They did not speak English, so they peppered Bo Shwe with questions about me in their tribal dialect, he told me later. He did not translate their questions, or his replies to them, at the time. I looked through my daypack for something to share with them, and pulled out a crumpled yellow bag of peanut M&Ms.

'Famous American candy,' I told them. I handed each of them a brightly colored M&M. One young woman tentatively put the candy in her mouth, and bit it in half. She smiled, swallowed the tiny morsel and popped the other half in her mouth. Everyone else, including Bo Shwe, decided it was safe to follow suit, and they nibbled at their M&Ms as if they were eating caviar. A couple of them examined the chocolate-coated peanut interiors with great interest. I invited them to have as many as they wanted, and each of them carefully plucked one more candy from the bag.

One of the nuns asked how much the bag of candy cost, and they were wide-eyed with astonishment when I told them it had cost 130 kyat. I decided to leave the bag of remaining M&Ms with them when it was time to leave. Before we went, Bo Shwe took a photo of me with the nuns and a little girl from the village who had wandered in while we were eating. The nuns wished us a safe journey home, and asked Bo Shwe to come again.

The lunch break was a welcome respite. As we left the village to head back down the trail, I decided I had established enough rapport with Bo Shwe to ask about more sensitive issues in the military. He answered all of my questions, although often with brief replies. I am not sure if it was a language issue or he just did not want to go into detail. I suspected the latter.

Because the army had such a bad reputation, particularly since the bloody crackdowns of 1988 and 1989, was it difficult for them to recruit soldiers, I asked? How had they found so many recruits to keep growing the military machine? I knew about the forced enlistment of young men, but wanted to hear his version of the story.

Bo Shwe nodded at my question. He recounted how army units often swept into rural villages and demanded that the village headman offer ten fit, young men to join the service. The young men and their families dreaded the prospect, with mothers often crying and clinging to their sons as they were led away. Often the recruits, who were as young as fourteen years old, had to be taken by force. (Amnesty International has repeatedly cited Burma for the brutalization of child recruits.)

What about desertion from the ranks, I wondered. 'It happens, but it is no use,' Bo Shwe said. 'They will come back to the village, find you and catch you.' He crossed his wrists to signify imprisonment.

Soldiers were not the only ones drafted into involuntary service. Human rights organizations have documented numerous cases of adults and children being rounded up to work as porters for the military, carrying heavy loads on rough mountain paths for kilometers with little food and no payment. Bo Shwe told me he had seen young children, some only eight or nine years old, taken forcibly from their villages. They were frequently made to walk in front of the troops with their heavy loads, essentially acting as human detonators in regions that are strewn with landmines laid both by the Burmese army and insurgents. Bo Shwe said nothing when I asked if he had seen children die this way.

'Everyone in the army is afraid,' he said after a long pause. 'Afraid to speak out and afraid to refuse. They are watching you all the time.'

The fear that pervades the army ranks is heightened by the soldiers' isolation from the rest of society, both physically and psychologically. The resulting atmosphere of paranoia provides some explanation for how the military government was able to convince soldiers that the pro-democracy demonstrations by unarmed protestors that sprang up around the country in 1988-89 had to be violently crushed.

Many of the army units that crushed the pro-democracy demonstrations, in which an estimated 3,000 protesting students, monks and others died in 1988, were transported in to the cities from remote parts of the country. Some of the soldiers were reportedly given alcohol in advance of the attacks, and fired with eyes blurred from inebriation.

When I broached the subject, Bo Shwe said many soldiers supported the democracy movement led by opposition leader Aung San Suu Kyi. 'Many soldiers left their uniforms and went to the demonstrations to see her,' he said. 'I was there.' He beamed as he recalled attending a huge rally for the opposition leader in Upper Burma. 'In addition,' he said, 'many soldiers secretly voted for her' in the election of 1990.

Yet fear kept the soldiers from sharing their political views even with close friends. Bo Shwe recalled seeing enlisted men he knew at the rallies for Aung San Suu Kyi, but they did not acknowledge each other. 'We love her in our hearts, because of her father,' he said, in reference General Aung San, the national hero who pushed for Burma's independence from Britain. 'But we cannot say this to anyone.' (In late 1998 and early 1999, there were reports of entire army companies deserting from their battalions and voicing support for Aung San Suu Kyi. In some instances, deserters reportedly joined the insurgents who are battling the army.)

Bo Shwe had flinched at a few of my questions, but he rarely avoided a response. I asked him how the military had changed since he joined the ranks more than forty-five years earlier. 'When I was a young man, the army was a decent job,' he said. 'Today, the army is no good.'

As I reflected on our conversation, I was struck by the fact that, despite the fear and hardships, he had accepted his life as a soldier. I did not sense that he was a man riddled with guilt or remorse. In part, it may have been because he had never known any other kind of life. Part of it, too, may have been his ability to see situations as he wanted to see them.

The sun was getting low in the sky, and we had reached the outskirts of town again. Bo Shwe stopped at the gate of a Nepalese woman he knew. 'Namaste,' Bo Shwe waved to her, using the Nepali greeting.

The woman, whose garden was abloom with magnificent flowers, called us in for a rest and a cup of strong tea. After a couple of inquiring questions about me, she turned to Bo Shwe to gossip about Nepalese friends. Bo Shwe told me later that the woman's husband was a military friend of his who had died several years ago. He stopped to see her a couple of times a week.

We were almost back to my hotel now, and Bo Shwe decided to take a shortcut across what I first assumed was a field; several meters onto the grass, I realized we were walking down a golf course. At the bottom of the hill, a small party of golfers in brightly colored slacks and polo shirts was crossing a bridge with caddies scurrying behind them. One of the men broke from the group and marched up the hill straight toward us. As he approached, I saw that he was a tall, handsome man in his early forties.

I offered a 'hello', drawing a hostile glare from the golfer, as Bo Shwe snapped a salute. The golfer marched within three meters of us and continued on to a ball nestled on the edge of the fairway about five meters beyond. Once we were out of earshot, Bo Shwe told me that the angry golfer was the commanding officer of his last regiment. The course we had just strolled down was reserved solely for the use of senior military officers.

At the bottom of the hill, I parted ways with Bo Shwe. 'Very sorry about the officer,' he apologized. 'I am sure he didn't see you.'

Chapter 9

A Village Sacrifice

We turned off the paved road and headed down a deeply rutted red dirt track. The World War II-era jeep began bouncing in and out of giant, rough-edged craters, sending shock waves up my spine. The steep, twisting slope and large holes gouged from the road forced me to hold tight to the flimsy door (there was no dashboard), not only to brace myself, but also to prevent the door from flying open as one jolt after another pounded the jeep. It occurred to me that the original shock absorbers were never replaced on this jalopy. At times, we were moving so slowly that I could have jumped out and walked at a faster pace. My driver and guide, who was negotiating the path as if it was a maze, gunned the engine to coaxed his jeep up and over the lip of another deep crater.

Between jolts, I looked up to admire the lush countryside and fertile valley ahead. The morning sun was still soft on the vibrant green hills of Shan State. The air was cool and fresh, one of the delights of this region, and the scenery was in the kind of high relief that exists only in pristine, alpine environments.

As we rounded a bend, we spotted a group of eight Taungyo women on the dirt track ahead. The women, wearing long, brightly colored *longyis*, were on their way home from the nearest market town, a two-hour walk away. The rattan baskets on their backs were empty, since they were selling rather than buying vegetables this day. They had made it nearly back to the village before the morning sun was high enough to warm the valley.

We pulled up alongside the group and my guide, who spoke the Taungyo language, engaged in some teasing conversation with the giggling young women before he asked them to hop in back of the jeep. For a moment, they peered through his window at me, the blue-eyed, blonde-haired foreigner in the front seat, then climbed into the back without further encouragement. There was not room for all of them, but six managed to squeeze into a tiny space with their large baskets, giggling the whole time. The two that could not fit in back did not seem to mind walking the last several kilometers to the village, and they smiled as we pulled away.

The Taungyo are one of the numerous minority tribes living in rural areas of Burma, many of which are found in the hills that rise up along the country's flanks and merge with the Himalayan range in the far north. Shan State, a wild, sprawling territory bordering Thailand and

China, has a particularly diverse group of such tribes: they include not only the Taungyo, but also the Shan people, who subdivide further into several groups with their own dialects; Palaung, Pa-O, Intha, and others. It is estimated that there are twenty-seven major subgroups in Shan State alone. According to Burmese government figures, two-thirds of the country's forty-six million people are Burman, with the remaining one-third made up of other ethnic groups. However, independent observers have estimated the percentage of non-Burmans to be higher, noting that many non-Burmans have taken Burman names to gain better opportunities for education and employment.

Minority tribes have been considered separate from the Burman majority throughout Burma's history. Indeed, during the British colonial era they were allowed to remain semi-autonomous and never fell under the direct rule that was applied to other parts of the country. The sense of minority tribes' separateness continues to this day. Each of these rural groups has a distinct language, dress and customs. Their interaction with the majority Burman population is primarily limited to market days – when tribe members often trek for hours from the hills on foot to squat by the roadside selling fruit, vegetables or flowers – or encounters with the military.

And so I found myself in a jeep full of Taungyo women, bouncing down a rutted track towards their village. Conversation was nearly impossible, given the jolts we were experiencing, but everyone was smiling. As we entered the village, the road became too narrow even for the jeep, so we parked in the muddy front yard of a thatch house, guarded by lounging water buffalo. My guide chatted with the women for a few more minutes before we bid them farewell and set out on foot.

There were about ninety households in this village. Most of the houses, which were raised off the ground, were simple structures made of thatch, but a growing number of the Taungyo live in houses made of limestone bricks. The people made their living through agriculture: rice, cabbages, ginger, garlic and chilies grew in abundance in the surrounding fields. There was no electricity, and until recently, the villagers walked three kilometers to a water source. One of the biggest advancements here in recent years was the construction of a gravity-fed system that brings water for drinking and bathing from the hills to a series of wells around the village.

Despite the basic living conditions, I could not help thinking this village presented a picture of idyllic country life: brilliant carpets of red chilies drying on woven mats in the morning sun, water buffalo lying about, a few small children darting at play, fresh mountain air, and quiet. The village was nearly deserted the morning we visited, in fact, since most of the people were already at work in the surrounding fields.

I had come to meet the village headman, Min Maw. The role of head-man, or village elder, is time-honored in Burma, a carryover from the administrative system that existed under the Burmese kings until the late nineteenth century. Although the headman's influence has waned in more urban environments, he remains an important local authority on dis-putes, financial and moral matters in villages such as this one.

Min Maw was not home when I arrived, so I had a few minutes to look around the house while his son, tall and lanky, went to find him. It was a simple, three-room thatched house on stilts. The plank floors were worn in each of the modest sized rooms, which included a kitchen, a living/sleeping room, and a storage room. In the kitchen, smoke from an open fire on the floor drifted up to swirl around strips of meat hanging from a wooden rack that was suspended from the ceiling before drifting out the nearby window. In the small side room, a sturdy black bicycle was propped against the door.

In the main room, where I was sitting, the only furniture consisted of a few bamboo chairs, with a low table set between them. Large woven sleeping mats, called *hpyas*, were rolled up and stood lengthwise in the corner. There was a faded black and white portrait of Aung San, hero of Burmese independence and the father of Aung San Suu Kyi, hanging on one wall. Family photographs were tacked up around it. Another wall was covered with oversize calendar photos of beautiful young Asian women, and brightly colored posters of kittens, both favorite decora-tions in homes throughout the country. Behind me, a small Buddhist shrine sat on a ledge next to a drawing of *nats*, or spirits of nature. A bowl of bananas and coconut was set in front of the shrine as an offer-ing.

The belief in spirits was apparent throughout the house, where dried leaves and branches hung over every doorway to assure that the house-hold *nats* would not interfere with family life. Other such spirits were believed to inhabit the fields, the forest, the water, and so on. Belief in *nats* is not restricted to the hill tribes in Burma, and often coexists with Buddhism in families as a kind of 'second religion', albeit a less formal one. Despite past attempts by Burmese kings and others to wipe out spirit worship, it has never been eliminated. Particularly in the hill re-gions of eastern Burma, tribes that have no other religious beliefs look upon the *nats* as beings to be feared, and given regular offerings. This Taungyo village was primarily Buddhist, evidenced by the monastery on the outskirts of town, but *nat* worship was clearly a part of the residents' everyday lives.

Min Maw arrived. At seventy-one years old, he had a dark brown, deeply lined face and a stubble of gray beard. He was wearing a white and yellow towel wrapped around his head, a blue and green checked *longyi* and military-green work shirt with the sleeves rolled up to reveal his tattooed arms. His eyes were deep brown and watery. The wrinkles at the corners of his eyes suggested this was a man who has spent much of his life in the sun. He chose his words carefully, and despite the smile in greeting, there was a tinge of sadness in his face.

I was told this man's village had experienced things I should know about. A Burmese friend had let him know of my interest, but I was cautious about raising any sensitive topics too soon, and follow his lead in the conversation early on. We exchanged pleasantries and he offered my guide a hand-rolled cigar. Tea was served, and we discussed several improvement projects underway in the village. The conversation was in Taungyo, with interpretation provided by the guide.

Then Min Maw began a story that quickly transported me from this idyllic scene to what seemed like another world.

In 1991, the military government had forced the people of this village, along with numerous other minority villages like it, to work on a new railway line being constructed in an area of Shan State that was several days' walk from their homes. According to Min Maw, at least one hundred people from his village were required to serve at a time. Their task was to clear brush, cut trees, build earthen banks and lay rail track, working with little more than hoes and their bare hands, on a six-kilometer stretch of the railroad. Other villages had been assigned to build other sections of the rail line. The laborers lived in thatched huts at the work site, since it was too far from their village to return home at night.

The timeframe that they were given to complete the task – eighteen months – seemed challenging from the outset, yet there were other setbacks along the way. At one point, 'we finished a two-mile [3.2 km] stretch of earthen bank and then the government changed the rail route, so we did it all over again', he recalled.

The laborers were given neither food nor medication, and had to provide for themselves. A few village women went along to cook for the entire group, but people could only eat when they were told to, and soldiers beat anyone caught eating at other times. Exposed to relentless rains in the monsoon season and the cold winter nights, a number of villagers fell ill. 'Fortunately, no one from our village died' on the railroad, Min Maw said. Other villagers were not so lucky.

Soldiers oversaw all of the work, often forcing the people to begin without breakfast in the morning and sometimes working late at night. Min Maw recalled one incident when a few exhausted young men resisted a demand to work late in the moonlight, and one of them wrestled an army officer to the ground. Soldiers immediately surrounded the young man and beat him senseless with their rifles. Village girls were occasionally raped by the soldiers.

It was Min Maw's responsibility to decide who in the village worked when. He assigned villagers to go to the work site in turns, one hundred per week. 'As the deadline got closer, the whole village had to go,' he said, 'even children and people who were not able-bodied. We had to finish by the target date.' As village headman, he alone was unable to leave the work site throughout the project.

He paused, and a pained look passed over his face. 'My wife died during the time,' he said quietly. 'I was unable to come home and be with her until it was too late.'

At the outset, the military had promised this village – indeed, all of the minority tribes forced into labor on the railroad – a variety of building materials as compensation for their efforts: one hundred sheets of plywood per village, as well as zinc and cement. The promise was never met. Instead, Min Maw was paid 10,000 kyat (slightly more than one person's average monthly wage in Burma) for the work of his entire village over eighteen months.

While the villagers were away, their fields were badly neglected. Production was only half of normal during that time, Min Maw said, and weeds covered much of the farmed area. Once the railway project was completed and the villagers returned home, it took two years for the fields to recover. The headman was thankful, however, that the fields were not more seriously affected: the rail line they were ordered to build crossed through the fields of other villages that received no compensation for their land and the damage to it.

The forced labor project had lingering effects not only on the fields, but also on the village's spiritual life. During the grueling days on the railroad there was no time for religious festivals, an important element of life for Buddhists, and when the villagers returned home they had no money for such things. 'It wasn't until the third year that we began to recover,' Min Maw recalled.

The suffering of this Taungyo village is by no means unique. Tales of forced labor at the hands of the military are rife throughout Burma. The Burmese use the term *loh ah pay*, which translates literally as 'voluntary labor', to describe these activities, but as Min Maw made clear, the people have no choice in such matters. Forced labor has been used to construct numerous roads, railways, dams, monasteries, and other major infrastructure projects, often drawing the criticism of international observers and human rights organizations. In the western part of the country, for instance, the forced labor of villagers and convicts was used to build a 500-kilometer long railroad line in Sagaing and Magway divisions, which included a tunnel dug through a mountainside. After the project was criticized in a United Nations report in 1995, the Burmese government claimed it had paid the laborers, but those interviewed two years later said they had received no compensation.

While many of the most extreme cases of forced labor have occurred in remote areas of the country among the minority ethnic tribes, city residents have not entirely escaped the call to work. For instance, residents of Mandalay, the country's second-largest city, were forced in recent years to contribute their labor to the rebuilding of Mandalay Fort, now a popular tourist destination in the city center. Mandalay residents told me that the only way to avoid working when one's turn came was to pay someone else to go in your place. The government has contended that residents are happy to 'contribute' their labor to such projects.

The most extreme cases of forced labor today occur in rural areas where the military has a large presence. This is the case in Shan State, due to past and continuing insurgencies by Shan rebels in the eastern hills and an ongoing battle against the drug trade. Burma produced an estimated 2,600 tons of opium in 1997 – enough to make more than half the heroin available in the world – and much of the opium was grown in Shan State. The government claims it has eradicated a significant percentage of the land under cultivation, but Western officials have cast doubt on those claims. Most of the opium is under cultivation by members of the minority ethnic tribes, who have used the drug money to finance both their daily needs and fund rebellions against the government. Where the military and minority tribes interact, tension remains.

At least for the time being, the most brutal times seemed to be behind this particular Taungyo village, yet Min Maw said the villagers still suffered a series of indignities at the hands of the military. Villagers are required to provide 'voluntary service' once a week to weed the grounds of nearby military compounds. In addition, the military demanded 1,500 kyat as a donation for fertilizer in order to 'beautify' their compound.

The military infringes on life in other ways as well. 'Soldiers come and poach from our land, cutting trees and bamboo,' causing erosion problems, Min Maw said. 'They cut the green trees instead of the old ones, for firewood and their houses.' They also steal ginger, chilies and cabbages from the villagers' fields.

'When I reported this to the regimental officer, he told me it wasn't so bad, and besides, I should be grateful to the soldiers for protecting our country from foreign invaders,' Min Maw said.

The military has also supplemented its human porters with horses and mules to haul supplies, and has demanded that local minority villages supply the animals. Min Maw's village contributed two animals worth about 10,000 kyat apiece.

Given the hardships, did young people want to leave the Taungyo village, I asked him. 'Where would they go? In the cities, they're treated as second class citizens,' he said. He laughed when I asked how the villagers were treated when they went to the nearby market towns. Everything about these people sets them apart from the majority Burman ethnic group, including their faces, their clothing, and their heavy accents.

Occasionally, young men from Min Maw's village head north for the famed ruby mines of Mogok, Burma's largest gem-mining town, to seek their fortunes. 'Eight young men just left a week ago to try their luck in Mogok,' he said. 'Two others left two years ago, and they haven't returned yet.'

The lure of the gem mines, a major source of the world's rubies and sapphires, is a strong attraction for many poor people seeking to improve their plight. In towns across the Shan State and elsewhere, I encountered young men and women whose husbands and wives had headed north to dig in the mines, work as traders or do other jobs in Mogok. Sometimes, married couples only see each other once or twice a year. There were just enough stories of fortune to keep a flow of people heading for the mines, and they seemed to be more persuasive than the accompanying tales of prostitution and endemic drug problems. (In order to discourage all but the most determined foreigners from going to Mogok, the government requires permits, travel with an exorbitantly expensive state-approved tour company, and lodging in a costly hotel run by an ex-general.)

Most of the people in Min Maw's village, however, chose to stay at home and dream of a peaceful life without interference from outsiders.

The sun was high in the sky. Before I got up to leave, I asked about the tattoos on the inside of Min Maw's arms. A flower on the left arm was meant to bring prosperity, he told me. A set of squares on the right arm was to keep him from meeting enemies or con men.

And the eel-shaped tattoos inside both wrists? 'These will help me escape if I am ever held captive.' He paused a moment. 'Sometimes it works, sometimes it doesn't,' he admitted. 'It depends on your stars.'

Chapter 10

Minority Voices

We had bounced along for several hours in the back of a pickup truck on the winding dirt roads of northern Thailand and had just passed a third military checkpoint when one of my companions, an official in the Karen National Union resistance movement, turned to me and asked, 'Do you know how to swim?' The question caught me off guard. I nodded, and wondered what his words might portend. A day earlier, Saw Meh Doh had offered to take me illegally across the border from Thailand into Burma's neighboring Karen State, but he had not provided many details. As a disputed territory within Burma, Karen State is one of many regions that are off-limits to foreigners, so a clandestine entry was my only option. The thought that we might swim across the border had not crossed my mind.

'Don't worry, you probably won't have to swim,' Saw Meh Doh assured me. 'We just have to get across the river.' He was a very fit man in his sixties, and told me later that he had swum across the Moei River, which marked the border in this region, on many occasions.

When the pickup truck finally navigated a final series of switchback turns and came to a stop in a remote clearing outside a tiny Thai village, we set off on foot for the river. Saw Meh Doh and I were joined by Saw Htoo Po, another KNU member who hobbled along beside us due to his artificial left leg. When he was a young soldier, Saw Htoo Po had had his leg amputated just above the knee after he stepped on a landmine planted by the Burmese army, which has waged a long-running war against the Karen National Liberation Army, the KNU's military wing. Amputees were a common, sobering sight in the border region.

As we approached the riverbank, I saw two thin white cows lounging under a tree near the shore, as if they, too, were waiting to cross the river, which was about one hundred meters wide and with a swiftly flowing current. Saw Meh Doh whistled for a young man on the opposite bank, who jumped onto a crude bamboo raft and pushed it toward us with a bamboo pole, using his entire body to lean into the pole with long, slow movements. When he neared the shore on our side of the river, we removed our shoes, waded out up to our knees and climbed aboard the raft, much of which was submerged under several centimeters of water. To prevent Saw Htoo Po's artificial leg from getting wet, the wiry young raft man waded ashore, let Saw Htoo Po climb on his back, staggered to the waiting craft, and poled us across the river to a muddy bank on the opposite shore. The mountain ranges on either side of the river valley were lush, green, and deceptively quiet.

Thus I entered Karen State, one of the most disputed territories in all of Burma. The status of this region is such a delicate issue that national maps of Burma sold on the streets of Rangoon do not put a label on it. The Karen people have been seeking autonomy from the government of Burma for fifty years, led by the KNU and resistance fighters of the KNLA.

The precise number of Karen people in Burma is difficult to estimate. The military government says they number about three million, while the KNU contends there are seven million Karen inside Burma and several million more in Thailand. A significant percentage of them, perhaps as many as 30 percent, are Christian. The ethnic Karens' name for their land is Kawthoolei, which literally means 'country of the Thoo Lei flower', although KNU literature translates the name as 'pleasant, plentiful and peaceful country'.

Unfortunately, the territory has rarely been pleasant or peaceful since the Karen began their struggle for autonomy five decades ago. Since Burma gained independence from Britain, the military government has concentrated political and economic power among Burmans in the center of the country, while minority groups like the Karen have been treated as second-class citizens. A number of minority ethnic organizations, including the KNU, have sought the right to self-determination and establishment of a federal union in which all the states in Burma will have equal rights. Unlike other ethnic groups, however, the KNU has vowed to continue the armed struggle until it achieves its goals.

Between 1989 and 1995, seventeen ethnic minority groups across Burma negotiated cease-fire deals with the Burmese government, leaving the Karen and a few other groups in open rebellion. Human rights activists have charged that the military junta was motivated to negotiate the cease-fire deals after its crackdown on the pro-democracy demonstrations in Burma in 1988-89. The agreements essentially allowed a number of minority groups to engage in drug production and trafficking if they laid down their weapons, activists have contended. If they agreed not to engage in politics and not to join the democracy movement, they were allowed to retain their arms for ten years. As the agreements expire, the SPDC will have to decide whether to ignore the ten-year deadline or risk trying to disarm the groups. As recently as May 1999, the KNU (which has not pursued the drug trade) denied a government statement that it, too, was nearing a peace agreement with the junta.

For quite some time, a policy labeled the 'Four Cuts' has been adopted by the Burmese military against remaining insurgent forces. The policy aims to cut supplies of food, funding, recruits and intelligence to the resistance fighters. The Burmese government has also attempted to divide the opposition, and in late 1994 supported the establishment of the

Democratic Karen Buddhist Army (DKBA), a splinter group of ethnic Karen fighters that has sided with the government forces. The military has made such an aggressive assault in Karen State in recent years that the KNU/KNLA have been put on the defensive, hundreds of Karen villages have been destroyed or forcibly relocated, and tens of thousands of refugees have fled across the border into Thailand.

My purpose in joining Saw Meh Doh and Saw Htoo Po on this excursion was to meet and interview villagers from Karen State. Our unconventional border crossing was extremely tame compared to the experiences of most people I met in this region. It was a territory riddled with evidence of conflict, and the villagers had borne the brunt of it. I had seen KNU maps of the border area denoting burned out villages, land mine fields, and encampments of government troops, whose policy has been to undermine the KNLA resistance fighters by attacking Karen villages. Since the KNLA has started using guerrilla tactics and the cover of thick jungle to its advantage, the Burmese military has found villagers to be much easier targets for its attacks.

As massive as the Burmese army's activities have been in Karen State and other ethnic regions, the extent of suffering by minority tribes is virtually unknown in Rangoon or Mandalay. Details of military campaigns are unreported in the state-controlled media, which ascribes the military presence in the border states to security threats from insurgents.

One of the villages that we visited in the border region was typical of those in the area. All of the 5,000 inhabitants had lived in the village less than a year, having either been forced from their homes deeper inside the country, or having fled in advance of army offensives. Although the houses in this village were built in traditional Karen style – open-sided thatch and bamboo huts built on stilts – the village layout was not typical for a Karen settlement, revealing the precarious existence of its inhabitants. Instead of being scattered about, the homes were built close together in neat rows. 'We decided it would be easier to escape and to count people in an emergency,' one of the village elders explained.

Finding enough food to feed the village inhabitants had been a challenge. Many of the people had arrived here hungry, since they were forced to abandon the crops they had planted in their home villages and had been hiding in the jungle for weeks or months before arriving here. Hillside rice cultivation, which most of the villagers had traditionally relied upon in the mountainous terrain, follows a rigid schedule through the year that cannot be interrupted. In an attempt to start a new rice crop in this border village, the people had used traditional slash-and-burn methods to clear the nearby hillsides, but they were wary of venturing far from their homes for long. They had also planted a large garden of cabbage and onions near the village center.

The Burma Border Consortium, an aid coalition dedicated to helping people along the border areas, had provided the villagers with some basic food assistance, but the village leaders were clearly insistent that the people not become dependant on aid. As we walked through the village, we saw families sitting cross-legged on the floors of their huts eating midday meals of plain white rice and, in some huts, a few green vegetables.

'We need to teach the people more about healthy diets,' Saw Meh Doh said, 'but there is so little to offer them.'

The story of sixteen-year-old Ghay Wah was typical of those that the villagers told us. We came upon the girl as she sat on the raised floor of a hut working diligently at a simple wooden loom. She was weaving a white dress with bright pink decoration, a traditional outfit for unmarried Karen women. She turned her clear, round face to greet me with a shy smile, but never stopped weaving as we talked. She spoke in the Karen language, and one of the village men acted as an interpreter.

Ghay Wah said she and her family were farmers who had been living peacefully in a Karen village of thirty homes about one day's walk from the border. Eight months earlier, the Burmese army launched an offensive in the area. A neighboring village was attacked by the troops one afternoon, and word arrived in her village that the government soldiers were advancing. Ghay Wah was at home with her parents and four younger siblings at the time.

'We heard shooting and saw smoke,' she said. 'Army troops were seen just outside our village. The elders ordered all the young people to leave immediately. They were especially worried about the young women and girls, for fear that we would be raped by the soldiers. Our family decided to flee. My parents tried to take a few things with us, some clothing and food, but we left many things behind. Of course we had to leave all our cattle, chickens and pigs.'

'We were so frightened,' she continued. 'We all ran together, but it was difficult because of my younger brother, who was only six years old, and my little sister who was an infant. The others were ten and thirteen years old, so they were old enough to run. We hid in the jungle for a couple of weeks. We met some other people from our village, and they told us that all the homes in the village had been burned down. Some of the men were taken by the SPDC and forced to work for them as porters. They had to walk in front of the troops to check for landmines on the path, which is very dangerous work. Others were beaten badly, but fortunately no one died.'

At that point, Ghay Wah's parents decided to cross the border into Thailand with their young family, hoping they would be safer there. It was the rainy season and the Moei River was high, so they had to use some of their meager savings to pay for a boat across the river. Once they arrived in Thailand, they settled in a Thai Karen village near the border. After only two months, however, that village was attacked in a cross-border raid by the DKBA. At that point, the family moved back across the border into Burma and settled in the village where I met Ghay Wah. They had been living there for five months.

When I met the young woman, she was alone caring for her one-year-old sister and looking after the family's few belongings. Her parents and three other siblings had left a few days earlier to return to their home village to determine if it was safe to move back there, eight months after it was burned down. 'Of course we want to go back, that is our home,' Ghay Wah said. 'But only if it is safe. I do not want to see the soldiers again.'

Thirty-two-year-old Saw Lay Ghaw was another Karen villager with a painfully familiar story to tell. The Karen farmer had been working in his fields with his twenty-year-old brother one morning when government troops suddenly emerged from the jungle nearby. The farmers immediately dropped their tools and began running, but the younger brother tripped and fell. 'When he got up, the soldiers immediately shot him,' Saw Lay Ghaw said. 'They shot him in the leg, and then again in the back, but he kept moving. Finally, he collapsed and died on the path to the village. Because all the villagers ran away ahead of the soldiers, we did not find his body until a week later, when we snuck back and buried him.' Saw Lay Ghaw's family, including his pregnant wife, his mother, and two young children, lived in the jungle for several months after their village was attacked until, nearing starvation, they hiked over the mountains to the border region.

Stories like those of Ghay Wah and Saw Lay Ghaw are common among the ethnic Karen and other minority tribes in Burma. Human rights organizations have documented thousands of cases of killing, rape, extortion, looting, forced labor, and forced relocations in Karen State and other areas dominated by non-Burman ethnic groups, based upon first-hand interviews with villagers and refugees. Reports published by the Karen Human Rights Group and the Shan Human Rights Organization, among others, have presented numerous accounts of the atrocities committed in Burma's rural areas. In some of the documents, the victims' names, ages, professions, and home villages are presented in neat lists next to the chilling details of their deaths: 'killed by mortar shells and grenades', 'burnt to death', 'raped and killed', 'beheaded' were among the entries I found. Some of the victims were as young as eleven years old.

The Burmese military strategy has typically been to launch an offensive in a target region, then force the villagers in that region to relocate into military camps or military-controlled areas. Once the villagers are under their control, the military typically uses them as porters or as forced labor to build roads, new camps, or other infrastructure projects. So many people have nearly starved and fled the work camps, however, that many villagers now immediately run away and hide in the jungle when the military moves into an area, according to human rights monitors. They estimate that tens of thousands of people today are living a fragile existence in the remote jungle areas of Burma.

The presence of armed resistance movements is apparently not the sole reason for the military crackdowns in remote areas of the country. The strategy of relocation, repression and forced labor has been pursued in many regions where there has never been armed resistance against the government, and in regions where the insurgents have reached cease-fire agreements.

The total number of people affected by the military activity in eastern Burma's troubled states is difficult to calculate. The largest number of people have been subjected to forced relocations. One human rights organization that closely monitors the region estimated the number of villages destroyed or forcibly relocated at 1,500 in Shan State, 400 in Karen State, and 200 in Kayah State. Another relief organization working along the Thai border with Burma estimated that as many as 300,000 people had been forcibly relocated from their homes in the eastern regions by 1998. Less information is available about remote western regions of the country, but increased military control in Chin State and Sagaing Division has also resulted in documented cases of forced labor and extortion in those areas.

For those villagers who escape direct attacks or forced labor, land mines are another hazard. All parties to the conflict in Karen State – the government troops, the DKBA, and the KNLA – have laid numerous mines along village paths and in fields throughout the region. The number of deaths and injuries from the mines has soared in recent years. In a sign of how a semblance of order has emerged amid the violence and suffering, several workshops have been established in the border region to make prosthetic limbs for land mine victims. Thousands of prostheses have been distributed over the past ten years.

I asked Saw Htoo Po, who lost his own leg to a land mine in 1986, if the injury had changed his view about the KNLA's use of the mines. 'We are using guerrilla tactics, so we need to use land mines,' he said. 'I have never felt regret. I am proud that I lost my leg. It means I sacrificed for my country.'

I told him about a young girl I had met the day before who had stepped on a mine in a rice field and had her leg amputated above the knee. What do you tell the children, I wondered? The father of four paused a moment before replying. 'I try to tell them that we have an obligation to serve all Karen people, and sometimes that means we have to make sacrifices,' he said. 'If we don't continue this fight, one day all our Karen literature, our culture, and our Karen people will be finished.'

Despite their setbacks in recent years, the KNU leadership, which is dominated by an 'old guard', has retained a firm grip on power. While the KNU leadership has insisted that it is not negotiating with the junta, some elements within the organization have called for dialogue to accompany the armed resistance. As Saw Meh Doh told me, 'At first, we thought fighting alone was the answer. Now we notice that negotiations and talking are the means supported by most people. But if you talk to a military government without military power, they will never listen to you.'

Saw Meh Doh, a devout Christian, attributed his faith for the inspiration to continue the long-running struggle. 'God wants us to learn something,' the KNU official told me. 'I believe he is doing things step-by-step. If we had won our struggle in a short time, we would have believed it was because our weapons and soldiers were superior to those of the enemy. Now, the people know that is not true. If we win through fighting alone, we would believe we were superior to other ethnic groups. But now, we realize that we have to work together with our brothers and sisters in Burma if we are to succeed.'

❧

After spending time in a refugee camp along the Thai border, I understood why one foreign human rights monitor called such camps 'a last resort' for many minority people from Burma. Yet tens of thousands of people have been living in camps for years, some of them since the early 1980s.

Mae La, the refugee camp that I visited, is the largest camp near the Burmese border in Thailand. The Burma Border Consortium reported that as of February 1999, 32,465 people from Karen State were living at Mae La, which blankets a series of cascading hills about one hour's drive north of the Thai town of Mae Sot. The camp's refugee count had increased by 355 people from the month earlier.

Walking through the camp, I paused at the home of Mi Thu, a twenty-eight-year-old Buddhist Karen woman with three young children. Her family had spent almost four years at Mae La after fleeing from their home village ahead of Burmese government troops who were rounding up villagers to perform forced labor. After hiding in the jungle for a month, the family walked to Thailand with a group of other people from their village.

Mi Thu and her husband had once grown rice on hillside paddies. 'Here, we have no work and we live on food distributions,' she said. I asked if they planned to return to their village someday. 'If the authorities can arrange it, perhaps we will go,' she said. 'If there is peace and tranquility, of course. But this decision doesn't depend on me.'

The bamboo and thatch homes inside Mae La camp are built on stilts, in traditional Karen style, but they are all within a few meters of each other and form a chaotic jumble of structures without any discernible order to them. The homes have no electricity or running water. A series of wells dot the massive camp, but in the dry season when we visited, the wells were running low and people had dug pits to find ground water for cooking and bathing. A series of stream beds wind through the camp's rough and hilly terrain, and we crossed them by balancing precariously on narrow logs laying across them. During the rainy season, the streams are prime breeding grounds for mosquitoes and malaria is widespread in the camp.

Since refugees are forbidden to work outside the camps, I saw many people lounging in their homes during the day. Land mine victims with artificial legs were a common sight. Drug use in the camps has reportedly increased in recent years.

Due to cross-border attacks by the DKBA on refugee camps in recent years, a series of earthen shelters had been dug in the ground to protect the refugees. There had been shelling at Mae La camp for the two years prior to our visit.

'If there is military activity on the other side of the border, some of the people here cannot sleep,' said Thaw Thi Wah, a Karen medic working in a camp health clinic run by Medecins sans Frontiers, an international aid group. 'In the dry season, which is when past attacks on the camps have occurred, some people dare not sleep in their huts and go to the shelters instead. We dug trenches for the patients near the clinics, in case of an attack.' Thaw Thi Wah, a handsome young man who said he thought he was thirty years old (he was not sure), had lived in refugee camps in Thailand since 1984, when his family left Burma to avoid forced labor.

The Burmese military and DKBA have charged that the refugee camps harbor KNLA soldiers. Saw Meh Doh and Saw Htoo Po, the KNU officials who had accompanied me across the border, acknowledged that KNLA members had families in the camps and frequently stayed with them, but insisted that weapons were not brought into the camps anymore. I asked the two men, who usually lived in the camps with their own families when they were not in Burma, if they felt they were increasing the risk of attack by being there. Saw Meh Doh had told me earlier he was a target of the Burmese army and DKBA because of his position within the KNU.

'I need to be here to protect my family,' Saw Htoo Po replied as Saw Meh Doh nodded in agreement. 'It would be more dangerous if I were not here. Besides,' he added, 'my children are in school in the camp.'

The opportunity for children to attend school is one of the few advantages of life in a place like Mae La. On the other side of the border, years of turmoil inside Karen State have prevented thousands of children from receiving any formal education. At Mae La camp, Karen children are provided with officially sanctioned education through primary school, which is compulsory for children in Thailand. A foreign aid organization has established a high school at the camp as well.

The availability of health-care services is another advantage of life in the camp over life in Burma's troubled border states. At Mae La, for instance, Medecins sans Frontiers runs two in-patient clinics and two out-patient clinics, as well as four malaria research clinics. In total, the clinics treat about 300 inpatients and 4,000 outpatients per month. The most common ailments in the camp include malaria, acute respiratory diseases, and digestive problems such as cholera and dysentery. In addition, about 100 people per month are treated at a tuberculosis ward that also serves residents of neighboring villages. When we visited, the clinics were staffed by three expatriate doctors and two expatriate nurses, as well as sanitation experts and approximately fifty local staff.

Land mine victims from Burma arrive at the camp clinic on a regular basis, according to Thaw Thi Wah, the young Karen medic. Such cases are sent to Mae Sot hospital for amputation, and then return to the clinic to be fitted with a prosthesis. 'Last week we had a thirty-year-old man arrive here,' Thaw Thi Wah said. 'He was a Karen farmer who stepped on a mine, and his friends carried him over the mountains to the border. From there, they got a taxi and brought him here. Unfortunately, he died of his injuries.'

In the early 1990s, there were between 80,000 and 90,000 refugees from Burma living in camps inside Thailand. In February 1999, the Burma Border Consortium reported 90,466 refugees from Karen State and 15,072 refugees from Kayah State living in Thai camps, as well as 9,895 people from Mon State living in resettlement sites. The total displaced population had increased by 1,859 from one month earlier.

'Up until a few years ago, refugees could come freely into the camps,' a relief worker based in Thailand told me. 'The whole situation changed after 1995. Once the DKBA was formed and it started attacking refugee camps, the camps were moved farther away from the border and consolidated.' The shift uprooted tens of thousands of refugees, and some of them have yet to be properly resettled. At a Karen refugee camp designated K9, for instance, she decried 'horrific conditions where people have been living under plastic for two years'. The camp is located near a controversial gas pipeline that multinational companies have constructed to pump Burmese gas to Thailand.

Statistics from the refugee camps do not tell the entire story of displaced people from Burma's border states. Human rights observers have estimated that more than 100,000 people from Shan State have crossed into Thailand since 1996, the year that the Burmese military began large-scale village relocations in the state. But the Shans were not placed in Thai camps, as other minority groups from Burma had been.

The human rights observers noted that the Thai government has developed closer ties to the Burmese junta in recent years, with a particular focus on trade and investment opportunities. As a result, they contended, the Thai government has not wanted to open new refugee camps that might call attention to repressive practices in Burma; rather, it claims that the people from Shan State (and other recent arrivals from Burma) are illegal migrant workers seeking better economic opportunities in Thailand.

A look at the history of the Shans in Thailand sheds further light on the situation. Unlike the Karen, the Shan people are ethnically related to Thais, as well as to Laotians. As a result, Shan refugees leaving Burma were welcomed by the Thais as early as the 1960s, and they were allowed to settle in Thai villages. Refugee camps were not an issue then, since there was little concern over the settlement policy. Today, however, the historically relaxed Thai policy towards the Shan is under strain because the number of Shans in Thailand has increased dramatically at a time when Thailand, struggling with its own economic problems, is not in a position to absorb them.

In addition, the historic links between Shan resistance movements and the drug trade have reportedly raised concerns within the Thai government that it not appear to be harboring drug traffickers or their supporters by placing Shan people in refugee camps. (That rationale was scoffed at by one eminent Shan leader, who charged that the Thai government simply could not admit that it previously had a policy that was friendly towards Shans and antagonistic towards Burmans.) The US government has particularly active programs in the region aimed at monitoring and eradicating the drug trade.

As a result, the Shan people who have poured into Thailand have had to fend for themselves as migrant workers. 'Once again, we face the curse of Shan State,' sighed a relief official in Thailand whose organization aids Shan people along the border.

While the KNU and KNLA have continued their armed struggle for autonomy from the central government in Rangoon, other ethnic minority groups in Burma have adopted less confrontational approaches to the government.

The Shan Nationalities League for Democracy is one such organization. The SNLD placed second behind the NLD in the 1990 general election in Burma, winning almost half of the legislative seats up for election in Shan State. Although the election was immediately annulled by the military government, the result gave the SNLD a legitimacy among ethnic minorities in Burma that has endured through the 1990s. In addition, the organization has gained added importance in the country since several armed Shan organizations – the Shan State Army, the Shan State National Army, and the Shan Democratic Union – have declared their support for it.

During a conversation with an SNLD official in early 1999, I heard a different perspective on minority issues than I had heard from the KNU. In an office adorned with photos of a historic meeting of Shan leaders, the SNLD official, a stout, jovial man in his fifties, outlined the three priorities for his organization.

'Our first concern is the economy,' he said. 'We want our share of trade and investment.'

In select frontier regions of the country, the military government has reportedly poured billions of kyat into development projects over the past decade, in an apparent effort to turn cease-fire agreements with insurgents into permanent peace. In the Wa region of Shan State (which is outside the SNLD's traditional area of support), for instance, government funds have been used to build roads, bridges, schools and hospitals. But observers generally believe that integration of border areas into Burma's economic mainstream will take many years.

The SNLD's second priority is for social improvements. 'Socially, we are hard up,' the party official said. 'Our schools have been closed down and our health facilities are in need of improvement.' Such issues are of concern throughout Burma as the faltering economy has resulted in funding cutbacks, but minority ethnic areas have been particularly hard-hit.

Finally, the Shan official pointed to his organization's political aims. The SNLD has become a representative supporting the interests not only of ethnic Shans (there are at least six million in Burma), but of all non-Burmans, in the government-convened National Convention that has met on-and-off since 1993 with the ostensible goal of drafting a new constitution for Burma. There are many who doubt the value of the Convention proceedings, but currently it is the sole forum for multi-party discussions in Burma. The NLD, among other parties, had walked out of the National Convention because it was undemocratic in its procedures, and the military has already been guaranteed a large portion of seats in any future parliament, as well as any presidency, so its predominance will be assured. 'Politically, we are deadlocked,' the Shan official said when I asked about the status of discussions on minority rights at the Convention.

The SNLD has been careful in its handling of the autonomy issue. 'In 1947, to gain independence for Burma, General Aung San came up to Shan State and we were promised secession,' the Shan official said. In fact, the Shans, (and other ethnic groups like the Kachin and Chins) were promised *equality*. Shans and Kachins were given constitutional rights to secede after ten years if approved by a referendum.

Shortly before the military coup that would alter the course of Burma's history, the Shans spearheaded a movement that advocated federalism and called for a legal constitutional amendment as an alternative to secession. In 1962, General Ne Win claimed federalists were trying to break up the country and he lead a military coup to seize power. That event was the beginning of the military rule that continues in Burma to this day.

In the 1990 election campaign, the Shan official said, the SNLD chose to avoid the issues of autonomy and equal rights in its platform, and to focus instead on discussions about improving the lives of the Shan people. 'We knew the time was not right,' he said. 'To avoid all these confrontations, we just went forward with our nationalistic movement. Frankly speaking, the Shans never wanted secession. They only wanted equal rights.'

Today, he advocates a federal system for Burma. 'Federalism is just equality,' he said. 'But the military government has been saying for thirty or forty years that federalism means the dissolution of Burma.' The United Nations has suggested a tripartite dialogue between the military government, the NLD, and the minority groups in Burma as a first step toward settlement of the nation's political disagreements. 'We will not forget this chance,' the Shan official declared.

Part of the challenge in starting any dialogue is that the military junta has actively sought to divide and conquer the opposition parties in Burma, including minority parties and the NLD. 'If the minorities were to join hands with the NLD, that is when you would hear gunfire again,' the Shan official predicted. 'The government doesn't want us to get along.'

Large areas of Shan State have also been dominated by drug production and trafficking that has strained relations between various political and ethnic groups in the region. 'Some of these groups are beginning to cooperate with the Thai drug authorities,' the Shan said, 'but unfortunately, many people are still governed by hatred and mistrust.'

Despite the challenges that Burma faces, both in general and in regard to its ethnic minorities, he made a final appeal to the international community to retain political and economic pressure on the Burmese government in an attempt to force change. 'As we go into the twenty-first century, the world is moving toward democracy,' he said. 'Please don't leave our country behind.'

Chapter 11

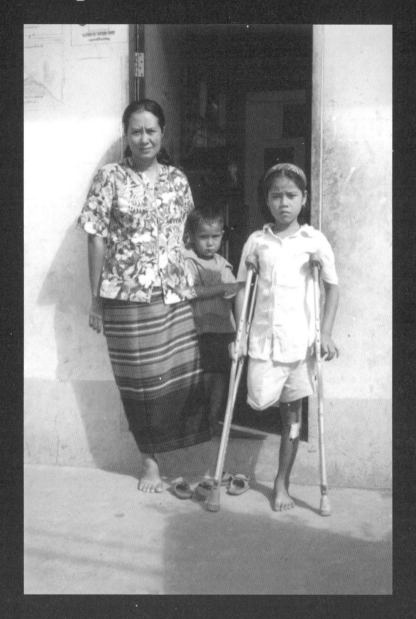

Where Have All
the Doctors Gone?

D r Cynthia Maung's health clinic is so well known that people will literally cross national borders to be treated there. It is a testament to the absence of modern medical care in much of Karen State that sick and injured people have walked, been carried, or dragged for kilometers over mountainous terrain to the clinic that this ethnic Karen doctor established on the outskirts of Mae Sot, Thailand, in 1989.

The Mae Tao Clinic, which is four kilometers from the border with Burma, was initially started in a small building to treat Burmese students fleeing the crackdown on democracy demonstrations inside Burma. Dr Cynthia herself had fled her hometown of Moulmein in Burma during the political turmoil in 1988, leaving so quickly that she did not have time to say goodbye to her parents. The young doctor joined a group of students and other Karen people who walked for seven days through the jungle to reach the Thai border. She has not returned to her home since then.

Today Dr Cynthia is a soft-spoken, middle-aged woman with a slightly weary air who has established such a caring reputation among the Karen people in the border region that another local doctor calls her 'Mother Karen'.

When Mae Tao Clinic was established, Dr Cynthia was primarily serving the thousands of Burmese students who congregated in and around Mae Sot, many of them suffering from malaria and wounds acquired in the jungle. Since then, the clinic has expanded into a health center with inpatient and outpatient services, maternal and child health programs, an eye care clinic, infant nutrition and immunization programs, and family planning counseling, serving primarily illegal Burmese migrant workers in the border area. It is staffed by three doctors and sixty health-care workers. Care is provided free of charge.

A walk through the original clinic building, which was dark despite a bright afternoon sun outside, revealed Spartan rooms, narrow hallways, and the powerful smell of excrement. I passed by the delivery room, which was separated from the hallway by a piece of chicken wire. Four hard metal tables, covered with thin plastic, were lined up a meter apart. The tabletops were only slightly over one meter from the ceiling above. To keep up with the clinic's growing patient load, construction had started on a new inpatient facility that was due to open in late 1999.

In addition to its patient services, the clinic trains traditional birth attendants in the border area to use modern methods, and sponsors mobile medical teams and backpack medics that travel throughout Karen State on foot to provide basic medical care in regions that are too unstable to support permanent clinics. A doctor who has traveled with the backpack teams said some of them walk as far as 650 kilometers before returning to their base in Thailand.

In 1998, the Mae Tao Clinic's inpatient and outpatient departments handled 19,471 patient visits, a 27 percent increase over 1997. 'More people are crossing the border as the government troops gain control of new territory' inside Burma, Dr Cynthia said. 'We are seeing more land mine victims, and more people need blood.' The number of blood transfusions at the clinic increased almost 300 percent in 1998 over the previous year. The clinic staff donates most of the blood given.

The most common ailments of patients at the clinic are acute respiratory infections, malaria and anemia. But a glance through the clinic's annual report revealed other medical problems that point to the difficult circumstances in which Burmese migrants live along the border. They included beri beri, tuberculosis, sexually transmitted diseases (including HIV), complications from abortion (such as hemorrhage and infection), and malnutrition.

An indicator of the nutritional health of migrants in the area is provided by the results of child nutritional assessments that the clinic started in mid-1998. In the first six months of the program, more than 2,200 infants and toddlers were assessed. Of those, 60 percent were found to be suffering from mild to severe malnutrition. Through the clinic's infant nutrition program, the children are weighed and fed a balanced meal once a week. Severely malnourished children are fed six meals a day in the inpatient feeding center.

Dr Cynthia is often called upon to serve as spokesperson for the clinic, since it frequently receives foreign visitors, including many from the relief organizations, Christian groups, and foreign embassies that provide grant money and support. The flow of foreign visitors is likely to increase since Dr Cynthia won the first Jonathan Mann Award for Global Health and Human Rights in June 1999. The thirty-nine-year-old Karen doctor, who earns no salary and lives in poverty with her family, was selected to win the US$25,000 award from among fifty international candidates. The Mann Award was named for a Harvard professor, internationally known AIDS researcher and human rights advocate who was killed in a plane crash in 1998.

I sensed that she was not entirely comfortable in a more public role, but the doctor agreed to sit with me for an hour one afternoon to discuss the social problems facing migrants in the border area. Her voice was low and tired, but her quick round brown eyes showed her interest in sharing the plight of the Karen community.

She noted that illegal migrant workers from Burma are frequently subjected to low pay and mistreatment by employers in Thailand. Entire families work on farms, in factories, or at construction sites. The use of drugs (particularly amphetamines) has reportedly increased among the migrant workers, some of whom believe the drugs will allow them to work longer and harder.

The Thai government has launched a crackdown on illegal workers in the border regions in recent years. Immigration officials in Mae Sot reported that more than 39,000 illegal workers from Burma were arrested and repatriated from four Thai districts along the Burma border in 1998, and another 15,000 were sent back between January and May 1999.

Among those migrants from Burma that remain in the Thai border districts, Dr Cynthia said, young women have particularly suffered. Prostitution is rife in the border area, and unsafe abortions are common among women who are afraid of losing their jobs due to pregnancy. Dr Cynthia's clinic frequently treats the complications of unsafe abortions performed elsewhere.

'Traditionally, the family structure has been very close in Burma,' said the doctor. 'But decades of economic hardship have had an impact. In Burmese families, tradition says that if there is a problem in the family, it is the girls who leave school to work or take care of the younger kids. They are usually the first victims.'

With an infant resting on her hip and two other young children hovering behind her skirt, the woman stood in the doorway of a smoky longhouse squinting into the midday sun. She was only thirty-three years old, but her face looked closer to fifty. Her eyes were dull and sad.

She welcomed us inside, and it took a few moments for my eyes to adjust to the darkness. Members of the Palaung tribe traditionally live in long, open rooms like this one, with several families sharing the same space. Open fires burned on the floor, and with no ventilation aside from a window at either end of the rectangular room, the air was choked with smoke. My eyes started watering almost immediately.

The woman's story was simple, she said. Her husband had come down with a bad cough a few weeks ago. She thought it was nothing at first, since he was normally a strong, healthy man. But he continued to lose energy, and eventually, was unable to get out of bed. At that point, several men from their village, a cluster of longhouses on a remote hilltop without running water or electricity, loaded him on their shoulders and carried him three hours over narrow, winding footpaths to the nearest hospital. The doctors said the illness was not too serious, but the patient needed bedrest and medication.

After the sick man had spent only one week in the hospital, his family ran out of money to pay for medicine and nursing care. At that point, the men from the village again trekked three hours to the hospital, loaded him on their shoulders and carried him back up into the hills. He died at home five days before our visit, at the age of thirty-four.

The story illustrates a couple of things about the healthcare system in Burma. The first is that remote minority villages often lack even the most basic medical facilities. The second is that Burma has a pay-as-you-go medical system. While beds in hospital wards are available to anyone for free, nothing else is. Patients and their families pay for medication, nursing care, physician fees and just about everything else. Only the poorest patients are provided with food, and others have to provide their own meals.

It is no wonder so many rural Burmese do not even try reaching a hospital. During our visit to the same remote village where we met the young widow, we were approached by a young man who said his father was very ill. I was with a friend who had spent several years as a medic in the Burmese army, although he had little formal medical training. The young man approached respectfully and addressed my friend as a 'medicine man', asking if he could do anything for the sick, old man.

'Where is he?' my friend inquired.

'Down there.' The young man pointed down and across a steep ravine to a tiny hut perched amid the thick foliage near the bottom of another hill.

We realized that a hike to the hut would take at least an hour each way, and it was already late in the day. My friend asked a few more questions about the old man's symptoms. He promised the worried son that he would be back within a few days with medicine. It would mean another full day of hiking up from and back to town.

'Where do you get the medicine?' I asked my friend.

'I'll buy it tomorrow at the pharmacy,' he replied. I knew his salary was only 2,600 kyat a month, and he could not really afford medicine for a stranger. We left the village, and during the hike back to town, I offered to join him at the pharmacy the next day.

The next morning, we met in the center of the town, pulling up on our bicycles at the same time from opposite directions. The pharmacy was on a corner, ringed by a high counter. Standing on the sidewalk, we could look right in to the shelves of neatly stacked boxes and bottles. A young woman in a white coat approached and asked what we needed. I had already told my friend that I wanted to pay for the old man's medicine.

He mentioned a few items to the pharmacist, and she returned a moment later with some antibiotics and a few aspirin tablets. 'Is that all?' I asked. The cost of these few items was less than 300 kyat. 'What else?' My friend was concerned that this is all too expensive for me, but I knew he would pay for it from his own meager salary otherwise. I kept prodding him until we had purchased a two-week supply of antibiotics, more aspirin, and a couple of saline drip bags.

I was leaving town the next day, so I was not able to return to the village with him. As he climbed back on his bicycle with the bag of medicine slung over his shoulder, he gave me a grin. He was going to make the three-hour climb back to the hilltop village the next morning. Not because it was his job, but because he wanted to help. 'Thank you,' he said. 'You may have saved the old man's life.'

A few days later, I met a physician in Rangoon and told her about the health problems in the remote tribal village. 'I feel sorry for those people,' she said. 'But few doctors want to go work in a village that doesn't even have running water. We have a hard enough time here in the city.'

'Nowadays, almost all the old pretensions and delicacies have been dropped. A doctor gives you an opinion and you ask him what you owe him, as boldly as you say "How much?" to a shopkeeper. But I can remember the time when you did not do that, when the pretense remained that the doctor's fee was an honorarium. You paid it rather furtively, and he received it with an air of surprise and gratification, like a present that was by no means demanded or expected. You will find that some of the older medicine men still behave in that manner; the younger ones simply take their money and make no pretense at all about it.' – Excerpted from a letter published in *The Working Peoples' Daily*, 30 June 1986.

A blotchy gray photocopy of the published letter, with handwritten notes scrawled in the margins and phrases underlined throughout its three pages, was handed to me by a physician on a steamy night in Rangoon. She gave it to me to read while she saw a patient in a tiny exam area behind a folding screen in her downtown clinic. No, she didn't write the letter, she said, but it highlighted an issue felt by every doctor in Burma. A profession that was once conducted in a revered and almost courtly manner has been caught up in the pay-as-you-go culture that has swept the country in recent years. With shortages in many areas, including medicine, and rising prices squeezing everywhere, it was inevitable that the medical field would be affected.

Dr May Si Oo saw about twenty patients a night in this one-room clinic, located on a busy avenue downtown. To reach the clinic entrance, one had to weave through racks of blouses and dresses set out on the sidewalk by a women's clothing shop next door. Dr May Si Oo, a solidly built woman in her late thirties, and her family lived upstairs.

The narrow clinic was brightly lit. The waiting area was lined with wooden benches, and large posters of roses covered the glass windows of some ceiling-high storage cabinets along one wall. On another wall, posters advertised 'Nerve Tonic for Hard Workers and the Elderly', and 'Lipochol – Liver Protector for Alcoholics'. Both products were made in Japan. The doctor's patients were a mix of ordinary working people from Rangoon, including shopkeepers, hawkers, and porters. They were the same people feeling much of the economic squeeze that has gripped the country in recent years, as prices rise and the kyat is devalued further.

'I use a sliding fee scale for my patients, but I have to guess what they can afford,' she said. Her consultation fees ranged from 100 to 200 kyat per person. For that sum, she would supply any immediate needs for basic medication. Injections cost more.

But she was clearly troubled about where to draw the line with patients in Burma's pay-as-you-go medical system, since in many cases, the financial issue prevented patients from getting the treatment they required. For instance tuberculosis, a common ailment in the city, required nine months of treatment, she noted. But she could afford to provide each patient with only two weeks' treatment for free. After that, she would send her patients to the market to buy their own medication.

The situation has been aggravated by a government restriction on black market medicine from China, India and Thailand, all of which were widely available and relatively affordable in Burmese markets. Chinese medicine, in particular, is considered cheap and effective by Burmese doctors. But under the new law, the medical shops can only sell medicines sold through 'proper channels', which mean government-controlled trading companies. The approved medicines, which come from countries such as Singapore, Malaysia and Indonesia, are considered good quality, but also much more expensive. For instance, ten capsules of a common penicillin antibiotic might cost 100 kyats on the black market, and 900 kyats if an 'approved' imported brand is purchased. The result, said Dr May Si Oo, is that 'we have to play tricks and hide Chinese medicine in the cupboard'. Many patients who have to buy medicine through official channels run out of money and discontinue the treatment before the illness is finished. The result is a group of doctors squeezed by a sense of professional duty on the one hand, and economic reality on the other.

The situation in Burma – constraints on doctors' ability to practice, the growing economic problems of patients, and perhaps most importantly, their own low pay – has prompted many doctors to leave the country, or to seek other, more lucrative professions. Dr May Si Oo said that of the 300 students who graduated with her twelve years ago from the Institute of Medicine, only about one-tenth are still practicing medicine in Burma. Many of her classmates have gone abroad, to the United States, United Kingdom, South Africa or other countries. Still others have remained in Burma but have changed professions. Those that changed careers – generally men – are now making significantly more money in trading or real estate. Dr

May Si Oo estimated that 60 to 70 percent of all doctors practicing in Burma are women.

To stem the flow of doctors leaving the country, the government has instituted new regulations in recent years. Since 1996, every medical school graduate is required to serve the country for at least three years in order to receive a diploma. Prior to graduation, each student is asked if they intend to stay in public service for the minimum three years, or for their entire career. If the answer is three years, they are frequently sent to do their service in the most remote corners of the country.

Dr Daw Tin Htway, a fifty-three-year-old physician and lecturer at one of Burma's medical institutes, recounted the story of one of her medical students who ran afoul of the authorities. 'He said he wanted to serve the minimum three years, and they posted him to a place in Kachin State that's so remote, it's not even on the map,' she said. 'The authorities told him it was a very sensitive place, for military purposes, and one of the generals said they wanted a doctor there. But he refused to go.' As a result, she said, the student was stripped of his medical degree and denied the possibility of going abroad. 'If there was a promise that he could have gone abroad after his three years, he would have gone to Kachin State,' she said. 'But there was no such promise.'

In an attempt to increase the number of doctors available in Burma, the national Minister of Health (a former intelligence officer who previously served as Burma's ambassador to France) has proposed reducing the length of a medical school program to five years from six and a half. 'They're rewriting the curriculum to shorten it,' Dr Tin Htway said. 'I'm not sure what they can cut out.' (The doctor shortage has been exacerbated since the country's four undergraduate institutes of medicine were closed with all other universities in December 1996 amid anti-government demonstrations by thousands of students. The institutes were finally reopened in January 1999.)

Another recent national initiative was the addition of fees for the several private rooms in each hospital ward. The rooms, which used to be free, now cost about 1,000 kyat per day. Extra nurses' fees are also charged for the private rooms. Income generated from the private rooms is distributed among other hospital staff. Most patients, however, cannot afford private rooms. In a typical ward at Mandalay General Hospital, for instance, four small rooms hold fifty patients, grouped by sex and type of illness, to the extent possible.

Dr May Si Oo recalled that when she worked at Yangon Children's Hospital in the mid-1980s, they would put three children in one bed. 'It was so crowded, we just didn't have the capacity,' she said. 'There were one hundred new patients a day, especially during the dengue season.'

Dr Tin Htway had similar stories of overcrowding. 'Sometimes the wards are extremely crowded, particularly in the rainy season when we have a lot of malaria patients,' she said. 'The families can come anytime they want, except for a couple of hours in the morning and afternoon. They can stay in the room overnight too, sleeping on the floor or on benches. If there are too many family members in the ward, some will even sleep under the beds.'

The sociable nature of the Burmese was evident in Dr Tin Htway's recollection of her work as a young doctor in a rural hospital in the far western hills. 'When I made rounds at night, it was like a festival in the ward,' she said. 'Family members were everywhere. They were all eating, and some of the men were smoking.' She acknowledged that it made her job as a doctor more difficult, but said the practice was so ingrained that she wouldn't think of banning families from the wards.

Dr Tin Htway wanted to dispel any notion that Burmese doctors all readily abandon their country. 'Everyone wants to work here, they want to serve their people,' she said. 'But the pay just isn't enough.' For instance, a senior professor at her medical school with thirty years' experience is on a fixed salary of 2,500 kyat a month. As a result of the low salaries, virtually all doctors have their own clinical practices to supplement their incomes. Dr Tin Htway is at the medical center from 8:00 to 4:30 each day, then runs a private clinic from her home every evening until 8:30 p.m.

The doctors also lamented the lack of training and advanced equipment available. It was particularly galling to them that the country's top military officers have access to the best doctors and have specialists flown in from Singapore to treat them.

Dr May Si Oo, who said she sorely misses the opportunity for advanced education, said she had applied twice for a government job, and was rejected both times. 'Those are difficult jobs to get,' she said. 'I passed the written exam, but not the personal interview. Maybe I didn't look submissive enough.'

Instead, she spent a short time at a cooperative clinic in the suburbs of Rangoon before opening her own small practice. The financial challenge weighed on her, she said, particularly as she faced the daily dilemma of how much of her patients' care and medication to subsidize from her own pocket.

'You can not expect to make money from a clinic like this,' she said. 'If you really want to be a good doctor in Burma, you have got to have another business too. If you really want to help people, you have to have your own money behind you.'

Because of the challenges, many doctors continue to leave behind Burma in search of better opportunities abroad. But their experiences have been mixed. Dr May Si Oo has two sisters, both research scientists, who left Burma to work in Japan. Although they both found decent jobs, others they know have been unable to find positions in their profession. 'They wash dishes and earn a lot of money,' Dr May Si Oo said. 'If I went to Japan, I would not mind washing dishes too.'

'These people are so stoic, they think it's their *karma* to suffer,' said a Westerner who is working on AIDS prevention in Burma. The statement reveals a lot about the challenges in effectively dealing with the AIDS virus in this socially conservative, heavily Buddhist country. The rate of HIV infection in Burma is soaring, now almost as high as that in neighboring Thailand, but prevention programs in Burma are not nearly as developed as those in Thailand.

'Thailand has some of the best programs in the world,' said a foreign aid official. 'Here, we're still fighting denial. It's the same problem as in Thailand, but a very different level of response.'

An unpublished study by Burma's National Aids Prevention Program put the number of HIV carriers at 500,000 in 1997, and even that figure is believed to be conservative. Rates of HIV infection among drug users in Burma are estimated to be at 90 percent. Yet the country is in denial. Official government figures on AIDS and HIV are wildly underestimated, according to doctors and health experts. (The government reported 13,773 HIV cases and 1,612 AIDS cases in 1996.) Government steps to address the issue have included jailing prostitutes and heroin addicts, and putting AIDS patients in quarantine centers.

The tone for the country has been set by the Minister of Health, who considers condom advertisements inappropriate. 'He says it is shameful, in our culture, to look at these kinds of advertisements,' a doctor told me.

Even Dr May Si Oo appeared slightly embarrassed when she told me that she had one patient with AIDS, hastening to add that 'he comes from a very clean family'. The man was infected with the HIV virus through blood transfusions, she said.

AIDS got a foothold among intravenous drug users in Burma in the late 1980s. The country's eastern hills form a part of the Golden Triangle, the world's largest opium poppy farming region and source of about 60 percent its heroin. Although the vast majority of drugs are exported, there is a long tradition of opiate use in Burma, particularly in the remote hill regions. The AIDS virus took hold when addicts began to inject refined heroin, rather than smoking opium. 'Shooting galleries', where dirty needles are frequently reused, sprung up along the border regions and the gem-mining centers of northern Burma.

A French doctor who has done AIDS prevention work in the remote areas of Kachin and Rakhine states told me about drug dealers who would inject a needle directly into an addict's arm, suck blood out through a tube directly into the dealer's mouth, where it was mixed with heroin, and then is blown back into the addict's veins. 'Virtually every one of those dealers is HIV-positive, and they're-spreading the disease to every addict they service,' he said.

'The drug situation is terrible,' said Dr May Si Oo, who had recently attended a conference run by the head of the national drug control effort. 'We heard that it takes an average of two hours to find drugs in the US, an hour and a half in the UK, an hour in India, and only half an hour in Burma.' (In 1998, the ruling junta announced that it planned to eradicate all opium production – an estimated 2,600 tonnes were produced in 1997 – within five years. But for years, the drug trade has been the basis of economic life for hill tribes in the Golden Triangle, and has financed many of their rebellions against the Burmese government. Eradicating the lucrative business is seen as a major challenge, and the US cut off aid to the Burmese government's anti-narcotics effort for political reasons during the turmoil of the late 1980s.)

According to Burmese doctors, the use of drugs, particularly heroin, has spread far from the remote hill regions, and today laps at the edges of the Burma's most elite neighborhoods and families. 'The sons of the VIPs are affected,' one doctor said. 'Drug use started out among uneducated people, but now all townships have drug addicts, including the most exclusive areas in Rangoon.'

The drug problem is even more acute in Mandalay, the country's major trading center. 'The raw materials come from Shan State, they're refined and pass through Mandalay to other places,' said a local physician. 'We see heroin overdose patients in the ward. Some of them are rich men's sons, and others are older rich people. Most of them are Chinese, and most of them are wealthy. We generally only see the overdoses. Addicts with less extreme problems are generally kept at home and out of sight.'

Enhanced drug enforcement programs in Thailand and China since the early 1990s have prompted the opening of new drug supply routes for raw opium and heroin. The drugs generally originate in Shan State, are transported to the plains around Mandalay, and then frequently pass through Chin State and Sagaing Division into northern India for shipment to world markets. Burma's problem with HIV/AIDS has spilled over into neighboring countries as well, with both China and India reporting high infection rates in areas along the Burmese border.

Although intravenous drug use remains the primary source of AIDS infection in Burma, sexual contact has transmitted the virus from drug users to the broader population. Prostitution is illegal in Burma, but underground brothels are common along the Thai border and in the northern gem mining centers. Increasingly, they are found in the large cities as well. The country's steps toward economic liberalization in recent years have resulted in the opening of nightclubs, some of which offer more than music and drinks. Most prostitutes are driven into the business by economic hardship.

Another factor impacting the spread of AIDS in Burma is the mobility of the population. Many people – truckers, traders, men who leave their families to try their luck at the gem mines – travel extensively. 'People are so mobile in this country, I can't believe it,' said a foreign aid worker. Increasingly, men who are infected pass the virus to their wives. Doctors say the majority of transmission occurs through heterosexual contact.

'In previous years, most of the patients we saw suffering from AIDS were men,' said Dr Tin Htway. 'Now there are more women and children, even infants. Most of the women are not prostitutes, they are the wives of men who travel.' By 1997, 15,000 children in Burma had been orphaned by AIDS, according to a UNICEF report. But efforts to increase awareness about AIDS have had limited results thus far.

'Education of the general public hasn't been effective,' the doctor said. 'They know about sexually transmitted diseases, but they do not fear them.' Condoms can be purchased on the black market, but many men resist using them.

In Mandalay, many of the omnipresent bicycle trishaws bear stickers declaring 'Stop AIDS' and trishaw drivers wear T-shirts with a similar message. Unfortunately the messages, created and distributed by well-intended foreign organizations, are printed in English, which few people in Burma understand. On more than one occasion, I boarded a trishaw and, as we cruised down the tree-lined streets of Mandalay, I pointed to the sobering message on the driver's T-shirt. He would simply smile back and keep peddling.

Part IV
Voices Of
Tomorrow

Chapter 12

Chinese Accents

A Burmese friend and I were sitting in an outdoor cafe on 19th Street, a narrow thoroughfare in the heart of Rangoon's Chinatown. I say cafe, but in fact, it was just a jumble of folding chairs and plastic tables that had been set out in a hodgepodge manner in front of a tiny, neon-lit Chinese restaurant. Dozens of little restaurants in this block had done the same thing, and the result was a veritable maze of furniture that took up nearly half the street. Neon signs touting Tiger Beer glowed overhead. The cluster of beer signs had caught my eye the moment we rounded the corner on 19th Street, seeming rather out of place against the dark Rangoon sky. Most Burmese do not drink alcohol.

It was nine o'clock on a humid Sunday night, and 19th Street was bustling. Nearly every table on the street was occupied, mostly by young Chinese men talking loudly and slurping down bowls of steaming noodles. At the next table, a rotund, middle-aged Chinese man wearing a gold bracelet had just tucked into an enormous pile of food in front of him. His wife, wearing more makeup than I had seen on any woman since I arrived in Burma, was twirling one of the large, ruby-studded gold rings on her fingers as she watched him eat.

The cramped little street in Chinatown reminded me of Hong Kong. It was more noisy, chaotic, and garish than most side streets in Rangoon. A series of mini-dramas were played out in close quarters, while curtains of laundry hung drying from the buildings above. Children noisily darted in and out of the tables, and an old man with a few long, wispy hairs growing from a mole on his chin sat alone watching the activity around him.

I noticed that my Burmese friend, who had come to Chinatown at my suggestion, was distracted. Quietly sipping his soda, he had his eyes glued to two young Chinese women on the other side of the street. The women, who appeared to be in their early twenties, were wearing high heels and brightly patterned *cheongsams*, the form-fitting, traditional Chinese outfits with a long slit up the side of the skirt.

The pair were going from table to table, trying to encourage patrons to order bottles of Mandalay Beer. They appeared to be a little unstable walking in the heels, and did not seem to be having much luck with the beer promotion. Most of their time was spent standing next to each other on the sidewalk, staring unsmiling at the passing throng, before they made another half-hearted round of the tables. The 'perky sales girl' concept was lacking something in its execution.

My friend suddenly turned to me with a distressed look on his face. 'It saddens my heart to see that,' he said, nodding toward the young women. 'We Burmese believe it is not proper for women to do such things.'

My friend is a well-educated urban dweller in his late thirties. I do not consider him particularly conservative by Burmese standards. Reflecting to myself how mild the women's behavior was compared to what I had seen in many other Asian cities, I pointed out that their promotion was fairly harmless.

'No,' he insisted. 'It is not right.' He was visibly upset. It was one of those moments when the culture gap between the generally modest, soft-spoken Burmese and the more flamboyant Chinese bubbled to the surface. As Chinese immigration, investment and influence in this country have grown in recent years, so has resentment among the Burmese.

I suggested that we go for a stroll through Chinatown. We paid the bill and wandered down to the corner, leaving the relative intimacy of 19th Street for a major boulevard. The street was a contrast between light and dark, between the row of neon-lit gold jewelry shops, and wooden carts set up in semi-darkness along the sidewalk at a humming night market. Vendors were selling Hundred Year-Old Eggs, and porcelain teacups from their carts, which were faintly lit by bare light-bulbs. There was a buzz, an energy level, that I had rarely found in any of the Burmese markets.

The voices around us were speaking different Chinese dialects. The crowds jostled and pushed us along, and soon we were lost in the flow of the night. My friend did not say another word about the Chinese women in their *cheongsams*. But when I asked later if he would return to Chinatown any time soon, he just shrugged.

The culture gap between the Burmese and Chinese may be apparent on 19th Street in Rangoon, but the gap is a veritable divide in Mandalay. A growing number of Burmese grumble that Mandalay has become a satellite of China.

'Mandalay is now an unclaimed colony of Yunnan,' one lifelong resident told me with obvious irritation, referring to the neighboring Chinese province. 'We Burmese are becoming second-class citizens in our own country. They are spending very lavishly, while we Burmese people are suffering from great inflation. They are paying for it all with black money, drug money.' His charges may seem exaggerated, but similar views are widely held among the Burmese in Mandalay.

It is ironic that such a change has happened here, in the former capital of Burmese kings and the center of traditional Burmese language and culture. But Mandalay, located at a bend of the mighty Ayeyarwady (formerly Irrawaddy) River, lies at a strategic intersection of the trade routes linking

China to the east, India to the west, and Rangoon to the south. It is this confluence that has brought Chinese goods, immigrants, and money to the hot, dry plains of Upper Burma.

To be sure, the Chinese have long been successful businessmen in Mandalay. In his book *The Burman*, first published in 1882, the British author Sir James George Scott (known in Burma as Shway Yoe) described 'the Chinaman, smooth-shaven and prosperous as always, whether gaunt and big-boned from Yun-nan and Szuch'uan, or sleek and sturdy from Rangoon and the Straits, defying the most greedy official to rob him of his profits, and drinking his tea and smoking his opium-pipe with supreme composure and good humor.'[1]

But the growing Chinese influence in Mandalay today is more powerful than anything seen in the past. Chinese immigrants flooded into northern Burma in the 1990s, riding the tails of a closer relationship between the Beijing and Rangoon governments. Mandalay now feels like it is literally fueled by Chinese money. The city center is full of Chinese-owned hotels, restaurants and new office blocks covered in tinted glass. There are burgeoning Chinese residential districts, full of gleaming new houses with satellite dishes on the roofs. One has the sense of a brasher, bolder city than ever existed in the past.

'When I first came to Mandalay in 1966, the area between 26th and 35th streets, and 78th and 84th streets was almost all Burmese,' a friend recalled. 'Now, most of the people there are Chinese. I don't know what kind of Chinese they are, but they have got money. Since nationalization in 1964, most Burmese people had no capital and could not open private businesses. Only the Chinese seem to have capital. They make investments and run businesses.'

I asked another friend in Mandalay, a soft-spoken, bookish man with liberal political views, about the typical Burmese reaction to the Chinese, many of whom have lived in Burma for several generations. 'All we Burmese can do is look at them, and yes, there is hatred,' he admitted. 'They cooperate with the authorities in running their hotels and restaurants, and the authorities protect them.'

It can be difficult to tell, at times, whether someone is of Chinese descent or not, since many ethnic Chinese have taken Burmese names (changing one's name is a common and easy procedure in Burma) and there has been intermarriage between the communities. 'The Chinese are wearing trousers, not *longyis*,' was the tip one Burmese friend gave me to differentiate between the two; a good indicator, I found, but hardly foolproof.

There is a widely held belief among the Burmese that most Chinese wealth is based on two of the country's major exports: opium and gems. 'Drug money' is frequently cited as the source behind one successful businessman or another in the city. Official information on the sources of funds is impossible to obtain, but there is evidence that China has been a major

---

[1] Shway Yoe, *The Burman*. New York: W.W. Norton & Company, 1963

distribution route for drugs coming out of Burma's Golden Triangle. None-theless, it is difficult to separate the Burmese claims about their Chinese neighbors' sources of income from a general resentment of relative Chinese affluence.

What the Burmese fail to mention is that the Chinese have also been hard-working and resourceful. As is the case throughout Asia, the tight-knit Chinese communities of Burma have helped their members with financing, pooling their resources and lending to help new businesses get started. Many of the early Chinese settlers came to Burma during the British colonial pe-riod. Unlike the Indians, who most frequently arrived with the British as civil servants and soldiers, the Chinese were traders and businesspeople. The first waves hailed primarily from the coastal provinces of China, often arriv-ing by ship. Most of them settled in and around Rangoon. During the nine-teenth and early twentieth centuries, the capital city's foreign population – Chinese merchants, Indian civil servants and British administrators – out-numbered its Burmese population.

Another group of Chinese arrived in Burma as a result of World War II. During and after their entanglements with the Communists, members of Chiang Kai-Shek's Kuomintang (KMT) forces sought refuge in the hills of northern Burma. From there, they organized and launched raids back across the border. When the KMT were ultimately defeated by the Communists, many soldiers chose to settle in Burma rather than return to China.

The 1960s were tumultuous years for all Burmese, but particularly the Chinese. Huge anti-Chinese riots in the mid-1960s left hundreds dead. Re-cent conversations with Burmese friends yielded a variety of explanations for the riots three decades ago (including the 'provocation' of Chinese stu-dents wearing Mao buttons), but there has been widespread speculation that the riots were instigated by the government to divert the Burmese peoples' attention from economic problems, including a controversial in-crease in the price of rice. Thousands of Chinese (as well as Indians) were stripped of their assets and forced to leave the country. Many were from families that had been in Burma for generations. Another wave of Chinese – and many other residents – left the country in the mid-1970s, following a popular uprising and subsequent government crackdown in 1974.

But today, the Chinese presence is clearly on the rise again. In a nod to the Chinese community's growing importance, the government allowed a Chinese-language newspaper to begin operations in late 1998, the first such publication in more than thirty years. (Before 1966, there were six Chinese papers in Burma.)

Many recent Chinese immigrants to Mandalay have come from Yunnan Province, which borders Shan State. Yunnan is a remote, landlocked and relatively undeveloped province by Chinese standards, but it is along the main supply route for goods coming into Burma. The movement of goods and people along that route has been closely linked to the sometimes-uneasy relationship between the two governments.

After the deadly anti-Chinese riots of 1967, Beijing's policy suddenly turned against the Rangoon government. China began supplying arms to Burmese Communist rebels, and relations between the countries turned frosty for years. In the early 1990s, however, after both governments had violently put down popular democracy movements, the policy shifted again. Seeking to stanch the flow of arms to the Communists, the military government in Rangoon essentially struck a deal with Beijing: stop supplying weapons to the rebels, and in exchange, gain greater access in Burma.

The result is evident everywhere from the streets, where Chinese-made military trucks haul supplies for the Burmese army, to the markets, where Chinese-made electronics, clothes, shoes and pharmaceuticals predominate. There are suggestions that the growing Chinese presence is more than economic. In 1998, just weeks before startling the world with unexpected nuclear weapons tests, the Indian government claimed that the Chinese had established listening posts on Burma's CoCo Islands in the Andaman Sea. Some observers wonder if China's ultimate goal in Burma is access to a strategic, warm water port for her naval fleet.

Whenever I raised the subject of Chinese influence with Burmese friends, most of them voiced guarded optimism that the Burmese government had the situation under control. A few said the government was walking a tightrope, playing the Chinese off against other Southeast Asian neighbors (and foreign investors), such as Thailand, Malaysia and Singapore. They pointed to Burma's decision to join the Association of Southeast Asian Nations in 1997, which reportedly upset 'big brother' China as a snub. (The economic crisis that began in Southeast Asia in 1997 has deflated earlier enthusiasm for that initiative.)

In some of Rangoon's intellectual circles, the Chinese threat is perceived as more cultural than political. 'I see Chinese, as well as Indians, infiltrating our culture,' a well-known Burmese teacher and writer lamented. 'They're introducing Chinese music with Burmese words. Don't get me wrong, I appreciate variety. But they will get the upper hand. The Chinese and Indians will eventually take over.'

For centuries, the Chinese have considered jade a highly valued stone. Some of the richest jade mines in Asia can be found in Burma's northern Kachin State, where jade has been recovered since the thirteenth century. Ironically, jade has never been highly sought after by the Burmese themselves, who simply call it *kyauksein*, or green rock. As a result, most of Burma's jade is exported to China.

In a dimly lit showroom on the southern side of Mandalay, I wandered among rows of glass cases full of green jade bracelets, necklaces and earrings. The cases were half-covered with tarpaulin. I passed through the showroom to get to the attached home of Yi Yi, a bouncy twenty-four-year-old Chinese woman who spoke excellent English. Her father owned the showroom, which supported a family of eight children, two parents and a grandmother.

Yi Yi said the stone came from near Myitkyina, in the northern state of Kachin. From there it was transported by truck or train to Mandalay, where workers in her father's factory produced thousands of jade bracelets, necklaces and earrings that ended up in the showroom before they were shipped off to Rangoon, and then points farther afield.

Yi Yi does not like wearing jade, even though she's of Chinese origin. 'Too old-fashioned,' she sniffed. 'My grandmother wears jade.' Indeed, she is a thoroughly modern young woman by Burma's standards.

Yi Yi was a zoology student at Mandalay University before the universities were shut down in late 1996. More than two years later, she was very bored and looking for escape. She spent her days visiting friends and, occasionally, traveling. When we met, she had just returned from a two-month stay with friends in Bangkok, and was eager to share her photo album. But first, she fetched me a can of cold Tiger Beer without even asking. It was the first time I had been offered anything but tea or coffee in someone's home since I had been in Burma.

As we flipped through the album featuring photos from Yi Yi's stay in Bangkok, it was clear that she had not captured any of the typical tourist sites. Instead, there was a photo of Yi Yi in her sunglasses and a short skirt astride an elephant, a series of shots featuring transvestites in drag (she and her friends visited a lot of nightclubs, she explained), and photos of a theme park with miniature versions of world-famous monuments like the Eiffel Tower and the Sydney Opera House. In every photo she appeared in, Yi Yi was wearing a short skirt and chunky-heeled shoes, which were all the rage among trendy young women in most of Asia's major cities.

Not so in Burma. 'My parents scolded me when they saw these pictures,' Yi Yi said with a grin. If she was looking for shock value at home, she could not have done much better than what she had displayed in the album.

Yi Yi was outspoken, independent and itching for adventure. 'I want to move to the United States or Australia,' she declared. 'What's the weather like in Los Angeles?' Her friends in Bangkok had introduced her to the diet food Herbalife, and she was interested in a sales job with the company in California. Obtaining a passport and permission to travel abroad, which is so difficult or impossible for many Burmese, did not seem to be a problem for her family. As with so many things in Burma, money could smooth the way.

It was clear that Yi Yi was bored with life in Mandalay. She complained that since the university had been closed, she and her female friends had had hard times finding jobs. 'It is much easier for the boys,' she said. A few of her friends had found jobs selling jeans in a brightly lit shop that also features baseball caps, watches, and shirts with fake designer logos.

When I asked what they did for entertainment, she briefly perked up in describing a former nightclub in one of the foreign-owned hotels. 'They had a great buffet there,' she said. 'Twelve dollars for all you could eat.' That was nearly twice the average monthly salary in Burma. The nightclub was shut down, however, after a drunken fight between two patrons, she pouted.

We were talking in the living room of her family's house, which was much larger than most homes I had been in. With its Chinese characters and good luck signs on the walls, it had a very Chinese feel. Yi Yi's eighty-year-old grandmother shuffled into the room with the help of two canes and a nurse supporting her. I immediately notice the old woman's tiny feet, bound up in ornately decorated slippers. Yi Yi dutifully jumped up to help her grandmother settle into a chair. Because the old woman was hard of hearing, her granddaughter practically yelled at her to be understood. Grandmother spoke Chinese.

I ventured a greeting in Mandarin. 'Ni hao, ma?' Grandmother's face immediately brightened. She was thrilled to meet a foreigner who spoke some Chinese. I learned that she was born in northern Yunnan province, and moved to a highland town across the Burmese border with her family as a teenager. It was there that she met her husband, a first-generation Burmese-Chinese. Once the young couple were married, they moved to Mandalay and had one son, Yi Yi's father. Grandmother's husband passed away years ago, and her days were now filled with her eight grandchildren, watching television and grumbling at her nurse, a pretty young Burmese woman who hovered in the background.

Yi Yi had been perched attentively on the arm of Grandmother's chair throughout our visit, chiming in with translation assistance when needed and yelling in the old woman's ear when she couldn't make out the words. They were a study in contrasts – the young perky woman who traveled alone, rode elephants, spoke English and visited nightclubs, and an eighty-year-old woman with bound feet who hardly knew any Burmese – yet it was clear they were close and, although they lived in Burma, they were very Chinese.

Chapter 13

The Next Generation

One sweltering afternoon, while wandering through a pottery-making village in the Ayeyarwady River delta, I came upon a group of tiny, barefoot children playing in the reaching shade of a tamarind tree. A couple of enormous water buffalo stood silently in the midst of their chattering games. The children, who could not have been older than three or four, immediately surrounded me and looked up with big smiles.

A couple of them grabbed my hands and began pulling me down a narrow dirt path, which led to a tin-roofed, open-air classroom, where I found one young teacher orchestrating lessons for sixty students of various ages. Their school abutted a row of six-meter-high golden Buddhas nestled into a low hillside, which formed a kind of natural wall along one side of the class. The students sat literally at the feet of the Buddhas as they recited their lessons.

I stood in the back for a moment, taking in the scene, until the teacher looked up and saw me. She did not speak English, but gestured for me to come to the front of the class and took my hand with a smile. 'Mingala ba.' The Burmese greeting literally means 'It is a blessing.' I turned to the students, who were simultaneously shy and curious to get a closer look at me.

Once I greeted the class, a few of the bolder boys at the back called out something that I did not immediately understand. Soon the whole class chimed in, and I realized they were yelling 'Shoes! Shoes!' in English. They were telling me to remove my footwear, in a sign of respect for the Buddhas. When I pulled off my sandals to expose two sunburned feet, the class erupted in laughter.

It is hard to miss the local school in most Burmese villages. Following the sound of young voices in the schoolyard, or the students themselves as they walk to class in their green and white uniforms, I paid several impromptu visits to primary schools. I was invariably invited in by the friendly young teachers, who did not seem to mind that my visits disrupted their overflowing classrooms. They were welcoming and gracious hosts, eager to introduce me to the children and, sometimes, to practice a little of their English.

The primary schools I visited were all in rural areas, and the facilities were extremely basic. The simple, one-room structures were either open-sided (in the humid south of the country) or had wooden walls without panes in the windows (in the north), and were jammed with rows of rough wooden benches and long plank desks. Sometimes, blackboards separated the sections for students in different grades as they sat in the same room. From the scrawling on the board, I noticed that some students were learning both the Burmese and Roman alphabets.

Most of the teachers were young women, who dutifully carried on under difficult teaching conditions. A Burmese friend who took me to visit a tiny village school said it was a challenge keeping these women in their posts in some of the more remote areas. 'They find boyfriends in town and get married,' he said. 'Who can blame them? This really is missionary work.'

But the true missionary teachers were expelled from this country a long time ago. I met a Catholic priest who vividly recalled the day in 1965 when government troops seized the school run by European priests and nuns in his town.

'The army came and surrounded the mission school,' he said. 'They surrounded it with their guns drawn, and seized it like an enemy encampment. All the children were inside, some of them only five or six years old, and they were terrified.'

At the time, he recalled, the military-backed government was in the midst of a campaign to 'nationalize' all the schools in Burma. All but the most elderly foreign missionaries, including French, Germans, British, Italians and Americans, were ordered to leave the country. The schools the missionaries built and ran for decades – many of them in areas populated with minority tribes that had adopted Christianity – were taken over by the state.

'"Nationalized" is a misnomer,' said the Burmese priest. 'No one was compensated. The government simply seized the property.'

The abrupt takeover of schools more than thirty years ago is one of the tragedies of the Burmese educational system that continues today. The country has a long, proud history of learning and once boasted a literacy rate of about 80 percent, but the educational system has been repeatedly whipsawed for political purposes since 1962.

Most recently, more than thirty universities and colleges, which have been closed by the government on numerous occasions since 1962, were shut down again in December 1996 after several weeks of student demonstration. They remained closed more than two years later, although there were reports they might be reopened in 1999. Primary and secondary schools did not escape the government's sweep. In 1997, they were closed for a normal spring vacation in March and did not reopen for five months due to government fears about unrest before Burma was admitted to the ASEAN regional trade group in July 1997.

Literacy statistics in the country also have been manipulated for political ends. When the government was seeking debt relief through designation as a *least developed country* by the United Nations in 1987, it reported that the literacy rate had dropped suddenly to 18.7 percent from 78.6 percent. Current reliable statistics are hard to come by.

Education in Burma is mandatory through the fourth grade, but a United Nations study has estimated that almost 40 percent of school-age children never attend school at all. Less than one-third of Burma's children complete primary school, one of the lowest rates in the world. In many cases, parents cannot afford the cost, which includes regular 'contributions' not only for uniforms, books and pencils, but also desks, chairs, and even teachers' salaries. Government education budgets were slashed in the early 1980s, while military spending soared.

The result is a nation of underpaid, under-equipped teachers and school administrators. The headmistress of a primary school in a large city told me she earned one thousand kyat per month. The forty-three-year-old woman, who had more than twenty years' experience in education, said her husband was forced to quit his job as a government teacher and become a private tutor because they could not make ends meet. He earns ten times his government salary in the tutoring job.

Nevertheless, the couple's income is still so low that they live with their teenage son in a one-room bamboo hut that is lit by a single, bare light-bulb. The night they invited me to their home for dinner, I sat on a rough-hewn bamboo bench in front of the narrow desk where the husband prepared his students' lesson plans. The desk doubled as a dining room table, for there was no other table in the house. He sat alongside me on the bench, under the glare of the light-bulb, and the wife watched us eat a meal that had undoubtedly cost them most of their combined monthly incomes. I knew it was the custom for women of the household to eat after their husbands and guests, but I urged her to join us, exclaiming at the large quantity of food she had prepared. She politely declined.

'We are so honored to have you in our home, please eat,' she urged. I was embarrassed to have the headmistress of a school treating me this way, but tried to be a gracious guest and thanked her again for the meal.

Her husband, the tutor, asked if I had ever worked on a computer. 'I have never seen one,' he admitted, 'but I think some of my students will use them in the future.' He had not heard about the Internet or email. As I explained their capabilities, I realized that this middle-aged man, who was considered one of the most educated people in his town, would probably never have the opportunity to use them. It was not so much a question of money, although he surely could never afford a computer, but rather a question of government control. In a country where long-distance phone calls and fax machines are still tightly controlled, it seemed inconceivable that email access would be allowed for the public any time in the near future.

'I cannot image communicating that way,' he said after listening to my explanation of email. 'It sounds like an amazing thing.' After a pause, he added, 'But you know, I would rather have you speak to my class in person tomorrow than send a message.'

In a tiny school down a deeply rutted road in Upper Burma, I encountered a young man with a gift for teaching. U Ba Than was tall and lanky, a dark-skinned man with a slow, steady smile. He was twenty-three years old, and had only a ninth grade education himself. About two-thirds of Burma's primary school teachers have no formal training, since they must work for several years before the government will invest in training them. The rural areas, where 90 percent of the nation's schools are located, are particularly lacking in trained teachers.

U Ba Than clearly adored his young charges. As a friend and I watched, he arranged a group of squirming, giggly five- and six-year-olds in a large circle in the schoolyard, had them join hands, and led them in a song about the virtues of Buddhism. Then they scattered, laughing and running.

The children at this tiny school came from several minority tribes – Shan, Pa-O, and Intha, among others – reflecting the ethnic diversity of this region. Some of them did not even speak Burmese when they arrived on the first day of class, but it is government policy that minority languages will not be taught in the schools.

One of U Ba Than's jobs was to ensure that the students would speak and write basic Burmese by the time they reached the fourth grade. But sometimes, those basic skills can take years to master: according to UNICEF, it takes more than twelve years, on average, for a student to successfully complete five years of primary school in Burma. Only a small percentage of children go on to middle or secondary school.

U Ba Than was clearly popular with his young charges. When he called them to go back to the classroom, a knot of the smallest children gathered around him, clinging to his legs almost as tightly as his *longyi* did. The teacher gently pried them from him and urged them to run ahead to their desks. 'We do not have much to work with here,' he said. 'But I can not imagine doing anything else.'

Today, the vast majority of Burma's primary schools are state-run. In addition, there are about 900 monastery schools around the country. The monastery schools, which were the backbone of the country's educational system until the early twentieth century, now train fewer than 1 percent of primary school students, many of them from families too poor to send their children to government schools.

In some parts of the country where there are significant ethnic Chinese and Indian populations, those communities have developed independent educational systems for their children. Chinese and Tamil schools were established by parents who believed their children could get better instruction, as well as cultural education, there than in the government schools. These schools, and a series of private tutoring classes for college-bound students that have sprung up in the cities, have created a kind of parallel educational system that has sapped the government school systems of many bright students in recent years.

Teachers and ex-teachers also lamented the caliber of students seen in their classrooms.

'We are poorer than our ancestors when it comes to education,' said a former high school history teacher. 'After the schools were nationalized in 1965, students' English skills deteriorated and they lost interest in world affairs. Students today do not have curious minds.'

The repeated government shutdowns of universities – a dozen times since 1962 – has had a particularly damaging effect on students, and created a huge backlog of others waiting to enter institutions of higher education.

'It is no wonder that most students are less interested in education than they once were,' said the former teacher, who taught for twenty-five years in a government school. 'They have no hope. But there are some who still want to pass their entrance exams with high marks. Their parents push them to do it.'

As if shutting the universities was not enough, the government dealt a further blow to student morale in early 1999 when it meted out particularly harsh sentences to students accused of orchestrating a series of street protests in Rangoon in late 1998. About 200 students were given lengthy jail terms, including one that was reportedly sentenced to fifty-two years in prison. Most of the other students arrested received sentences of seven to fourteen years. The harsh sentences were apparently meant to dissuade students from getting involved in political activities once the universities were reopened.

Students are not the only ones whose morale has been severely dampened. Teachers and university professors, who have traditionally been held in high esteem in Burma, have been targeted by the government in a series of measures meant to assure their cooperation with the party line and prevent them from engaging in political activity.

In 1991-2, thousands of teachers and several hundred university professors were dismissed from their jobs for holding views contrary to those of the military government. Thousands of other teachers were transferred around the country, and many were forced to attend 're-education courses' that focused primarily on political topics.

Some were less fortunate. The former high school teacher I spoke with was arrested and spent five years in solitary confinement in the early 1990s for his involvement with an opposition political party. 'They charged that I attended a meeting sponsored by the National League for Democracy,' he said. 'Yes, I attended, many people attended. But it was only an excuse. They felt I was a leftist and that concerned them, since I'm a teacher.'

He recalled the night the military officers came to his house to arrest him. 'As usual, they said they would only question me briefly, just for a moment. But it lasted five years,' he said. 'A moment in this country can last a very long time.'

'I know your voice,' said the elderly monk, a twinkle in his eye. I was surprised, to say the least. I had never met this man in my life. He lived in a simple monastery down a long country road in Upper Burma, and I had stopped in completely by chance.

'Yes, I know your voice,' he repeated, serving me a cup of steaming tea. 'I listen to the Voice of America every morning.' I realized that what he recognized was the American accent, although I was the first American he had ever met in person. Eager to use his English, he proceeded to comment not only on current events in the outside world, but also about former US President Abraham Lincoln, whom he had read about and particularly admired.

English-language radio services like Voice of America and the BBC World Service, both available on short-wave radio, are linguistic lifelines for millions of Burmese like the old abbot, who learned to speak English as a boy in monastery school. Not only do the programs bring news of the outside world to people entirely cut off from serious reporting (as opposed to propaganda) by their government, but they also bring regular contact with a language that once flourished in Burma.

The best English speakers in Burma today are people over age fifty who learned English as children in school or, in the case of the elderly, during the British colonial period. The most fluent among them attended either missionary schools run by foreigners, or the European Code schools, where English was the language of instruction and Burmese was taught as one subject.

All that changed in the mid-1960s, in the midst of the government's program to overhaul the Burmese education system, when English was banned from most classrooms nationwide. Even the widespread Anglo-Vernacular Schools, in which classes were taught in Burmese and English was offered as a regular subject, modified their curricula so English was not taught until the tenth grade.

Suddenly, a former British colony in which top students had occasion to study at Oxford and Cambridge, and names like Winston and Elizabeth were widespread in the classroom, found that English was no longer encouraged. Foreigners teaching languages were asked to leave the country, and with them went the ability for students to hear native speakers in the classroom. The teaching of English in the lower grades was not reinstated until 1980 when, according to a widely repeated story, General Ne Win's daughter was denied access to a British medical school because of her poor English skills.

Unfortunately, by then even the teachers had a hard time catching up. I met several English teachers on my travels in Burma whom I had a hard time understanding. The English ability of most people under age forty is poor to non-existent. I have had numerous conversations in the markets and temples with old women and men eager to practice their English with a foreigner, while their children and grandchildren looked on with total incomprehension.

But today, foreign languages are increasingly in demand. The partial liberalization of the economy since the early 1990s, and resulting trickle of foreign investment and new hotels, has created a market for people who speak foreign languages. English is the most popular language to learn, and signs for English-speaking classes are sprinkled throughout Rangoon. Mandalay, too, has several such schools. Japanese and French are also growing in popularity due the increase in tourists from those countries.

In Maymyo, the old colonial hill station now known as Pyin Oo Lwin, I encountered an English-speaking class on a weekend field trip. We meet at the Botanical Gardens, a vast expanse of manicured lawns, flowered gardens and a lake set on the outskirts of town. The park is like a little patch of England that was picked up and set down on the other side of the world. It seemed an appropriate place to visit with a class of English-speaking students.

Why were they studying English, I asked the students, who ranged in age from nineteen to twenty-three?

'The best jobs involve English,' said a bright-eyed young woman of twenty. What sort of jobs did she mean? In a hotel, or with a foreign-owned company. Most agree that they were studying English to get better jobs. A few said they would also like to travel someday.

None of them had ever met an American before, and I could tell I was being scrutinized from head to toe, particularly by the young women. They were taking in every detail of my face, clothing and hair.

'Do American women wear jewelry?' asked a young woman who was wearing a series of gold necklaces and rings, as many Burmese do. I realized they were forming their impressions of American women based on my rumpled appearance, and I told them that traveling in the heat and humidity of Burma, I was not dressed quite the same way I would be at home in the United States. There were smiles all around.

And did they understand me alright? 'Oh yes,' one young woman replied. 'You speak English very well!'

To get to the private tutoring class, I turned into a dark, narrow doorway on one of the colorful downtown side streets, and mounted a flight of steep, nearly vertical stairs covered in damp, threadbare carpet that was worn through to the wooden steps in many places. At the top of the stairway, a colorful jumble of sandals was piled in the narrow hallway outside the classroom door. The smell of cooking food – I could identify curry, onions, and shrimp paste – came wafting down the hall from an adjacent apartment.

I kicked my shoes onto the pile, and stepped barefoot into the classroom. About fifty teenagers were attentively sitting at rows of long wooden tables and benches in a room with high ceilings and framed paintings hung high on the walls. There were roughly an equal number of boys and girls. I noticed that the boys are all sitting on one side of the center aisle, the girls on the other. Their teacher, whose portrait hung prominently on the wall, was standing on a stage holding a microphone and lecturing.

I was visiting one of Burma's top tutoring classes, where serious students from upper-middle to upper-class families came to prepare for their university exams. This truly was the cream of Burma's student population. All of these students hoped to enter university (only 3 percent of Burmese students pursue post-secondary education), and all of them had abandoned the overcrowded, poorly funded, state-run high schools in their quest to do so. Instead, they spent their days in private classes like this one, or studying at home.

The private tutoring route is not a cheap one, by local standards: this class alone cost 500 kyat per month for one, three-hour class each week. Students generally have a separate tutor for each of the nine subjects they will be tested on in the university entrance exams: Burmese language, English, math, geography, history, economics, chemistry, physics and biology.

But in the eyes of these students and their families, the price is apparently worth it. A student's test scores on the entrance exams determine not only what university he or she will attend, but also what his or her major will be. The top scoring students generally pursue engineering or medical degrees, while those at the other end of the spectrum are assigned majors like zoology. The fact that all universities across the country had been closed for almost two years at the time of my visit did not seem to deter them.

The teacher stopped his lecturing to introduce me, a visitor from abroad, and invited me to step up on the stage, handing me the microphone. The students looked up expectantly. I asked how many of them had met an American before.

Not a single hand went up.

I had hoped to make my visit a little less obtrusive, so after a brief introduction of myself, I set down the microphone and started moving around the classroom, holding short conversations with individual students. Their English was halting, but they seem to understand me. The students closest to us listened intently to each of my one-on-one conversations, while those on the other side of the classroom chatted among themselves, welcoming a break from the lecture.

The students in this class were all seventeen or eighteen years old, and generally came from upper-class families. Their parents were engineers, lawyers and other professionals, part of a small elite in the capital city. The children of senior military officers attended similar tutoring classes.

On the boys' side of the classroom, I sat down next to Thaung Tin, an eighteen-year-old neatly dressed in a short-sleeve plaid shirt and sporting a digital watch on his wrist. He had been in the class for three months and hoped to earn 'distinction' in his exams, he told me. Thaung Tin wanted to be an engineer, and was clearly a serious student. He said he spent seven hours a day either in class or studying. In his limited free time, he liked to read Burmese literature. Did he have any other hobbies, I asked, movies or music perhaps? He glanced around for a moment and felt the eyes of his classmates upon him. 'I really don't like movies,' he said, 'and I rarely listen to music.'

On the girls' side of the room I first approached Kyi Kyi Ma, a very shy, young-looking seventeen-year-old who was hiding behind large-framed glasses. Her cheeks were dabbed with cream-colored spots of *thanaka*, a traditional cosmetic made from tree bark that is worn by many Burmese women and children. She looked down as I squatted next to her desk. Kyi Kyi, whose father was an engineer, said she hoped to follow in his footsteps. She was sinking lower in her chair, shrinking from the attention I was giving her. Math was her favorite subject, she said. Did she know anything about the United States, I asked? She looked up and smiled. 'Geography,' she said.

The girl sitting next to her, also seventeen years old, could not have been more different. Aye Aye Win spoke English very well, and confidently looked me in the eye. She had a round face, and a shorter haircut than most Burmese girls her age. She told me her mother was a lawyer who has essentially raised Aye Aye and two younger sisters alone, since their father, a seaman, was generally away for long stretches at a time.

'I want to study medicine,' she said. Yes, it was very competitive to be accepted to the medical institute, she admitted, and the course would last seven years. And what were her plans after university, I asked? 'I want to be a famous businesswoman.' She didn't seem to see anything unusual about studying medicine to pursue a career in business, and, based on what I had heard from Burmese doctors, would hardly be the first medical school student to make the same decision.

After my conversations with her studious classmates, I hesitated for a moment to ask Aye Aye about her interests outside of class. But when I did, her reply surprised me and made me smile. In her free time, Aye Aye said, she listened to 'heavy rock music, especially Guns n'Roses and Bon Jovi.'

My time with the class was running short, but I managed to ask one last question of this confident Burmese teenager. Was she interested in traveling abroad some day? 'Yes,' she said, without missing a beat. 'I want to go somewhere that I can be happy.'

Epilogue

My most recent visit to Burma was in the spring of 1999. At the time, the Western media was full of news about the US and European military campaign to end Serbia's 'ethnic cleansing' of Albanian Kosovars. The war in Yugoslavia was being covered by the official Burmese press as well. But rather than publicizing the plight of displaced and tortured Albanian refugees, the government-controlled media carried stories condemning the NATO attacks on Serbia and foreign interference in Yugoslavia's internal affairs.

I did not make any further connection between Kosovo and Burma until a few days after my arrival when I was interviewing an elderly man in Upper Burma. As we were about to part, he turned to me and asked, 'Are the rumors true? Is the United States military coming to save Burma next?' The old man lived a simple life in a tiny village and, after telling him I doubted such intervention was likely, dismissed the speculation as a case of small-town gossip gone awry.

But a few days later, back in Rangoon, I heard a similar question from a well-educated teacher who regularly listened to English-language broadcasts of the BBC World Service. 'I hate to bring this up,' he said, 'but I must ask you. I have heard that NATO is planning a mission in Burma when they have put things right in Kosovo. What can you tell me?'

The fact is, many people in Burma could not understand how the repression of ethnic Albanians in Kosovo could prompt an international military response, while the repression of millions of Burmese citizens was largely ignored by the rest of the world. Surely the West would come to Burma if they knew what was happening in our country, many of them speculated. I found it a hard question to answer when I was staring into the expectant face of a Burmese friend.

Part of the challenge in Burma is convincing foreigners that there is more to the country than gleaming pagodas, cultural treasures and smiling people. The strides made by the Burmese government in winning the propaganda war among foreign tourists was underscored for me on my most recent trip as I sat in the departure lounge of Rangoon airport waiting to leave the country. I was seated next to a Frenchman in his sixties who had just spent two weeks visiting Burma's best-known cultural landmarks with an organized tour group.

'How did you find the country?' I asked. 'It was delightful,' the Frenchman replied. 'It is one of the most wonderful places I have ever been.' He paused for a moment, and then added, 'They say this country has a nasty military dictatorship, but I find it hard to believe. Everyone seems so warm and happy'.

At the time of our conversation, twenty-eight elected representatives of the NLD were in prison, another seventy-five elected representatives were under house arrest, hundreds of thousands of ethnic minority people had been displaced from their homes, universities across the country remained closed after two-and-a-half years, and millions of ordinary Burmese were living under the twin burdens of economic hardship and political repression. Of course these things were out of sight of the tourists.

I agreed aloud with the Frenchman that the Burmese people were warm and welcoming, but I wondered to myself how so many of them kept smiling.

Glossary

All Burma Students' Democratic Front (ABSDF) Overseas dissident organization consisting of many former students that continues to advocate for democracy in Burma. A dwindling number of ABSDF members still wages the struggle for democracy from camps along Burma's borders, although they have renounced armed conflict in recent years.

Association of Southeast Asian Nations (ASEAN) A regional trade organization that Burma joined in 1997.

Aung San National hero who led Burma's struggle for independence from Britain and the Japanese, and the father of Aung San Suu Kyi. General Aung San was assassinated in July 1947.

Aung San Suu Kyi The leading opposition figure in Burma and daughter of General Aung San, she serves as General Secretary of the National League for Democracy and won the Nobel Peace Prize in 1991. She was placed under house arrest by the SLORC government from 1989 to 1995.

Bamahsan Chin The concept of 'Burmeseness'. Buddhism is an essential element.

Burma Research Society Founded in 1910, the Society was the country's leading scholarly organization dedicated to the research, documentation and preservation of Burmese customs, history, language and literature.

Democratic Karen Buddhist Army (DKBA) Splinter group of ethnic Karen fighters that has sided with Burmese government troops in the long-running battle against KNLA troops in Karen State.

Karen National Union (KNU) Leading resistance organization among the ethnic Karen people that has been seeking autonomy for fifty years.

Karen National Liberation Army (KNLA) Military wing of the KNU that has battled Burmese government forces in Karen State for decades.

Karma A Buddhist concept that links one's fate in life to the deeds of a previous life.

Kyauksein The Burmese term for jade literally means 'green rock'.

Kyaung Burmese word for 'school' and for 'monastery'.

Kyat The Burmese currency. In mid-1999, the official exchange rate was 6 kyat to the US dollar, but the black-market rate was 350 kyat to the dollar.

Loh ah pay Literally translated as 'voluntary labor', this is the Burmese term for forced labor, which hundreds of thousands of people across the country have performed under military supervision.

Longyi A traditional ankle-length skirt worn by most men and women in Burma.

Mingala ba Burmese greeting that literally means 'it is a blessing'.

Myanmar In 1989, SLORC changed the official name of the country from Union of Burma to Union of Myanmar. However, the name Burma is still widely used, particularly among supporters of the popularly elected National League for Democracy.

Nats Spirits of nature, which many Burmese believe inhabit places such as forests, fields, water, etc. Many people believe nats are to be feared, and make regular offerings to the spirits.

National League for Democracy (NLD) Opposition political party led by Aung San Suu Kyi that won an overwhelming victory in the 1990 national election, which was immediately annulled by the military government. Hundreds of party members were thrown in prison for years. In 1998 and 1999, the government again stepped up pressure on the NLD, placing hundreds of party members and officials under house arrest and forcing many of them to resign from the party.

General Ne Win The long-time military leader of Burma, General Ne Win first took power in 1958 and served until 1960 when a national election was held. In 1962, he led a military coup against the elected government of U Nu and seized power again, abolished parliament, established a Revolutionary Council, and started the country down 'The Burmese Road to Socialism'. He has been a leading figure in the string of military governments that has served since then. Although he officially retired in July 1988, Ne Win is still believed to wield enormous influence behind the scenes.

Press Scrutiny Board Established in 1962, the PSB is the government's primary censorship body and has wide-ranging powers.

Pongyi A fully ordained Buddhist monk.

Printers and Publications Registration Act A law that requires all publications and printed materials to be approved the government before printing or distribution.

Shan Nationalities League for Democracy (SNLD) Political party representing ethnic Shan people that placed second, behind the NLD, in the 1990 general election in Burma. Several other armed Shan organizations have recently declared their support for the SNLD.

State Law and Order Restoration Council (SLORC) The military junta that ruled Burma from 1988 to 1997. SLORC, which was widely condemned for its brutal crackdown on unarmed democracy protestors in 1988, changed the country's name from the Union of Burma to the Union of Myanmar in 1989.

State Peace and Development Council (SPDC) The military junta that succeeded the SLORC in 1997.

Tatamadaw The Burmese armed forces.

Thanaka A natural cosmetic made from tree bark that is commonly worn by Burmese women and children.

U Nu The first prime minister of independent Burma, U Nu served from 1948 to 1958, when he handed over control to a military government under General Ne Win. U Nu returned to power as a result of elections in 1960, but Ne Win seized control again in a military-supported coup in 1962. U Nu was arrested and held in prison until 1966, when he was forced into exile. He returned to Burma in 1980, and died in 1995.

Yok-thei pwe Marionette theater, which is widely considered the highest form of performance art in Burma.

Photo Credits

Chapter 1:
Government troops intimidating crowds going to hear Aung San
Suu Kyi speak, 1989
(Dominic Faulder/Bureau Bangkok)

Chapter 2:
Aung San Suu Kyi addressing a crowd in front of her home, 1996
(Julie Sell)

Chapter 3:
Students demonstrating during the pro-democracy movement in
Rangoon, 1988
(Anonymous)

Chapter 4:
A rare procession of monks demonstrating in Rangoon, 1988
(Anonymous)

Chapter 5:
A young girl and her mother prepare to participate in a Buddhist
ceremony at Shwedagon Pagoda, Rangoon
(Julie Sell)

Chapter 6:
A veteran marionette performer demonstrating his craft
(Julie Sell)

Chapter 7:
Evidence of the British colonial presence remains in Burma's
former hill stations
(Julie Sell)

Chapter 8:
Government troops marching on Army Day, 1996
(Dominic Faulder/Bureau Bangkok)

Chapter 9:
Elderly man from a minority tribe at a market in Taunggyi, Shan
State
(Julie Sell)

Chapter 10:
An elderly Karen woman and her grandson after fleeing to a
village near the Thai border
(Julie Sell)

Chapter 11:
An eleven-year-old girl who lost her leg to a landmine in Karen
State stands with Dr Cynthia Maung at her clinic
(Julie Sell)

Chapter 12:
A boy waiting to buy sausages in Chinatown, Rangoon
(Julie Sell)

Chapter 13:
Burmese children in an open-air classroom
(Julie Sell)

About the author

Julie Sell is an American writer who has been working and traveling in Asia for more than a decade. A former journalist with *The Asian Wall Street Journal* in Hong Kong and *The International Herald Tribune* in Paris, she has also had articles published by *The New York Times*, *The South China Morning Post*, and *National Geographic News Service*, among others. Educated at Mount Holyoke College, The London School of Economics, and Northwestern University, she is currently based in the United States after years living abroad. This is her first book.